THE UNIVERSITY OF MICHIGAN
CENTER FOR CHINESE STUDIES

MICHIGAN PAPERS IN CHINESE STUDIES
NO. 32

CHANG CH'UN-CH'IAO
AND SHANGHAI'S JANUARY REVOLUTION

by
Andrew G. Walder

Ann Arbor

Center for Chinese Studies
The University of Michigan

1978

*Open access edition funded by the National Endowment for the Humanities/
Andrew W. Mellon Foundation Humanities Open Book Program.*

Copyright © 1978

by

Center for Chinese Studies
The University of Michigan

Printed and bound by CPI Group (UK) Ltd, Croydon, CR0 4YY

ISBN 978-0-89264-032-4 (hardcover)
ISBN 978-0-472-03825-1 (paper)
ISBN 978-0-472-12784-9 (ebook)
ISBN 978-0-472-90180-7 (open access)

CONTENTS

PREFACE

Chinese Marxism is unique in the world communist movement for the theoretical and practical solutions it has offered for the problem of maintaining unbroken change in social relations after the initial establishment of socialism. For a prominent contingent within the Chinese Communist movement, it has been insufficient to redistribute the means of production and end the exploitative aspects of the old society. Production relations, which include for this contingent not only property relations but all social relations embodied in forms of distribution, enterprise rules and regulations, and economic coordination, must be continually transformed to eliminate all vestiges of class distinction. This transformation is to take place largely through the conscious effort of people who live these relations in their daily lives. All literature and art, reflections of these social relations, must be mobilized to help facilitate this transformation. Individuals inside and out of the Party who resist these continuous changes as being detrimental to the rapid development of a socialist economy or as being harmful to literary and artistic creativity must be struggled with politically so that these changes can move forward.

Chang Ch'un-ch'iao has been one of the more prominent theoreticians and practitioners of this stream of Chinese Marxism, and the January Revolution has become symbolic of efforts both to promote social and political change and to overcome resistance to these changes by prominent Party and non-Party figures. The study in this volume traces the shifting involvement of Chang in the Cultural Revolution in Shanghai and the social forces in Chinese society which, once set off by the Cultural Revolution, decisively altered events in the city. Chang emerges as a complex political figure--both instigator and suppressor of political conflict, alternately champion and enemy of rebellion--and is throughout a protector of the ideals of his branch of Marxism who singlemindedly pushed for their realization through a number of sharp tactical turns. The January Revolution not only reminds us that classes continue to exist under socialism, as Chinese Marxists are the first to admit, but it also highlights the fact that a socialist society is capable of generating contradictions and conflicts that are distinctively its own.

This essay has benefited considerably from unusually perceptive comments upon various drafts offered by Lowell Dittmer, Albert Feuerwerker, Kenneth Lieberthal, Michel Oksenberg, and Ernest Young. Two others responded generously to my requests for assistance: Hong Yung Lee by allowing me access to his index of Red Guard materials, and Lynn T. White III by providing material from his own research and by helping to clarify certain points of confusion. Perhaps most importantly, without Michel Oksenberg's stimulating leadership of our seminar on Chinese politics and his active encouragement of my fascination with China's radical political figures, my efforts would never have been channeled in this direction. This expression of gratitude in no way confers responsibility for this piece on those mentioned above. Remaining weaknesses are in spite of their efforts.

Two others contributed in various other, but no less important ways, to the completion of this study. Marlene Thom served as an enthusiastic and capable editor, and George Walder's constant stream of clippings from the Washington Post helped his son keep abreast of major developments in post-Mao politics with a minimum of effort.

Andrew G. Walder
Ann Arbor, Michigan
July 1977

ABBREVIATIONS

AS	Asian Survey
CB	Current Background
CCP Documents	Union Research Institute, CCP Documents of the Great Proletarian Cultural Revolution
CCRG	Central Cultural Revolution Group
CFJP	Chieh-fang Jih-pao
CNA	China News Analysis
CNI	China News Items from the Press
CNS	China News Summary
CQ	China Quarterly
CS	Current Scene
DSJP	Daily Summary of the Japanese Press
FBIS	Foreign Broadcast Information Service, Daily Report (Far East)
FE	British Broadcasting Corporation, Summary of World Broadcasts (Far East)
FEER	Far Eastern Economic Review
HMWP	Hsin-min Wan-pao
JMJP	Jen-min Jih-pao
JPRS	Joint Publications Research Service
KMJP	Kuang-ming Jih-pao
MPC	Municipal Party Committee
NCNA	New China News Agency
PCJP	Pei-ching Jih-pao
PLA	People's Liberation Army
SCMM	Selections from China Mainland Magazines
SCMM(S)	Selections from China Mainland Magazines (Supplement)
SCMP	Survey of the China Mainland Press
SCMP(S)	Survey of the China Mainland Press (Supplement)
SCPRM	Selections from People's Republic of China Magazines
URS	Union Research Service
URS Bio	Union Research Service Biographical Service
WGHQ	Shanghai Workers' General Headquarters
WHP	Wen-hui Pao

I

INTRODUCTION

Shanghai's January Revolution was a highly visible and, by all accounts, crucially important event in China's Cultural Revolution. Its occurrence, along with the subsequent attempt to establish a "commune" form of municipal government, has greatly shaped our understanding both of the goals originally envisaged for the Cultural Revolution by its leaders and of the political positions held by the new corps of Party leaders thrust upward during its course--most notably Chang Ch'un-ch'iao. At this interpretive level, the events in Shanghai seem to embody in microcosm the issues and conflicts in Chinese politics during the Cultural Revolution as a whole, while at the same time shaping our conception of what these larger issues and conflicts were. At a more general, theoretical level, however, the events in Shanghai provide us with an unusual opportunity (thanks to Red Guard raids on Party offices) to view the internal workings of the Party organization under a period of stress and to observe unrestrained interest group formation and mass political conflict through the press accounts provided by these unofficial groups themselves. The January Revolution thus provides us with an opportunity to develop better our more abstract, theoretical understanding of the functioning of the Chinese political system and the dynamics of the social system in which it operates.

At the level of interpretation a single theme--that the January Revolution was a victory of Revolutionary Rebels over an entrenched municipal bureaucracy actively resisting and/or suppressing the emerging movement--has dominated most writings on the Cultural Revolution in Shanghai.[1] Central to this interpretation are two assertions: that the Scarlet Guards colluded with the Municipal Party Committee (MPC) to fend off the Revolutionary Rebels,[2] and that "economism" and the ensuing economic breakdown of the city in early January 1967 was a deliberate attempt by the MPC to sabotage the Cultural Revolution and preserve its power.[3] In marked contrast with the portrayal of the repressive stance of deposed Mayor Ts'ao Ti-ch'iu is the conception of

1

Chang Ch'un-ch'iao as a "radical ideologue" who assisted the rebel struggle in order to create a democratic commune in Shanghai.

This image of Shanghai's "January Revolution" and Chang Ch'un-ch'iao's role in it is, in many respects, seriously misleading. First generated by Chang Ch'un-ch'iao's Shanghai media efforts between January and March 1967, this image was tailored to meet clearly specifiable and urgently felt political needs. It grossly minimizes Ts'ao Ti-ch'iu's support for the movement and adherence to Central Cultural Revolution Group (CCRG) policies, while villifying his legitimate concern to maintain civil order and industrial production in the midst of the mass movement. It ignores the real social and economic grievances that gave rise to "economism" and obscures the central role that CCRG directives and the Shanghai Revolutionary Rebels themselves played in touching off the economic paralysis of the city. This tailored image cannot admit that Chang's central purpose in the first months of 1967 was to restore production while simultaneously suppressing and redirecting mass political activity--a task for which (in February 1967) he had the support of no more than a minority of the rebel factions of Shanghai's working and student population. This depiction of the events in Shanghai during the early stages of the Cultural Revolution has contributed, in turn, to a number of common misconceptions about the political concerns of Chang Ch'un-ch'iao and those closely aligned with him, as well as about the meaning of "radicalism" in the Chinese political spectrum.

These misconceptions will no doubt be fueled by the current post-purge polemics designed to discredit Chang, his colleagues, and the political principles they held. Chang, despite the fact that he was a key figure in reigning in these very same disruptive Cultural Revolution tendencies, is now portrayed as one who instigated factional violence, encouraged efforts to "overthrow all" leaders, and who, in the summer of 1967, urged attacks upon army troops and seizure of weapons by mass factions.[4] While few observers will accept the official conclusion that Chang was in reality a rightist who opposed the Cultural Revolution, these characterizations mesh with the dominant impression of him as primarily a disruptive political force.

A re-examination of these interpretive issues will open up some new perspectives both on the Cultural Revolution and on Chinese politics and society in general. If we reject some of the previous interpretations of these political events and the roles of key individuals in them, we will be forced to generate new interpretations and explanations of our own. If we do not accept, for example, the interpretation of mass political factionalism and strike behavior as products purely of manipulation by municipal level elites, then we must explain this behavior by examining the real social grievances of different sectors of the population and the cleavages to which they gave rise. If, further, we do not accept the interpretation that municipal level elites opposed and restricted the course of the Cultural Revolution from the beginning, then we must explain their behavior by reference to the organizational context in which their decisions were made.

For the events in Shanghai we are gifted with a number of sources-- Westerners living and teaching in Shanghai, Japanese visitors, the press of the various mass organizations and fragmented interest groups, accounts of Municipal Party Committee meetings and telephone conferences, and the "official" local and national press--all of which, when pieced together and cross-checked, will enable us to begin the difficult task of specifying such an alternative explanation. We are presented, first of all, with an unusual view of the organizational setting of Chinese politics and of the influence that organizational positions, patterns of communication, poor articulation of goals, and a rapidly changing environment have on the behavior of political elites. We are provided, secondly, with an unprecedented glimpse at the undercurrents, divisions, and conflicts within Chinese society and with an indication of how these undercurrents can shape the structure of political issues and even constrain and influence elite political behavior itself. We aim, in short, not only to achieve a clearer understanding of the behavior of any single political actor like Chang Ch'un-ch'iao or of any single political event like the January Revolution but also to begin to develop perspectives that might potentially enhance our general theoretical understanding of the Chinese political and social system. Towards these twin interpretive and theoretical ends we direct our efforts in this case study of an individual and a city at a crucial point in recent Chinese history.

II

CHANG CH'UN-CH'IAO'S POLITICAL
AND ORGANIZATIONAL BACKGROUND

Chang Ch'un-ch'iao is perhaps best known outside China for his consistent concern with fostering continuing revolutionary change in Chinese society. Chief among Chang's concerns have been that the process of social change might be slowed and eventually reversed, either through the persistence of "liberal" influences in art and literature or through the continuing existence of nonsocialist practices in China's economy. Chang's efforts throughout his career in the Chinese Communist Party (CCP) have been directed towards preventing such an eventuality. By confronting Party and non-Party members alike, and by pressing for continual changes in economic organization, Chang has sought to further these political ends.

The concerns Chang exhibited during the 1975 "Dictatorship of the Proletariat" campaign to restrict continually the "bourgeois right"[1] were entirely consistent with the role he performed in the CCP from the very beginning of the People's Republic. Chang's duties as a Party functionary in Shanghai's propaganda apparatus had continually involved him in efforts to maintain the current political line through ideological reform of press and literary circles or campaigns against "rightists." This unique organizational position helped to shape Chang's conception of the tasks involved in building socialism in China. While other functionaries struggled to increase industrial output by collectivizing, reorganizing, and rationalizing industry and agriculture, Chang was primarily concerned during this early period with reforming rules, regulations, and ideas reminiscent of the old society.

Appointed managing director of the New China News Agency East China Branch in March 1950,[2] Chang had from the first been involved in local efforts to reform press and literary groups. In 1951 he sat on the East China Committee to propagate the study of Mao-thought and was involved in a similar effort the very next year to carry out ideological reform in Shanghai's press circles.[3] During this early period he was

5

reportedly active in both the anti-rightist and Hu Feng campaigns, directing criticisms towards movie actors, directors, and writers.[4]

As Chang moved up within the Party hierarchy,[5] his activities became more intimately linked with those of the first Party secretary of Shanghai, K'o Ch'ing-shih. His association with K'o was crucial in shaping his political concerns and activities over the next decade, and it provided him with his first opportunity to participate in national politics. It is this association with K'o, rather than Chang's much later, more widely known alliance with Chiang Ch'ing, that involved him in fights over national policy and steered him on a political course leading directly to his involvement in the Cultural Revolution.

K'o Ch'ing-shih was an early supporter of Mao's Hundred Flowers policy in the spring of 1957 and an equally firm supporter of the anti-rightist campaign that marked the July retreat from that policy.[6] His strong, consistent support of Mao's Tsingtao conference pronouncement that the revolution had to continue on the ideological and political fronts marked him as one of the reliable provincial leaders to whom Mao could turn for support in national policy disputes.[7] As part of this consistent support for Mao's policies, K'o employed the efforts of his local Propaganda Department. Yao Wen-yuan, for example, as part of the "anti-rightist" campaign, attacked the "bourgeois rightists" of Shanghai's Wen-hui Pao for being too critical of socialism during the Hundred Flowers period.[8] Immediately following the anti-rightist campaign, in 1958, Chang Ch'un-ch'iao himself authored an article in Shanghai's Chieh-fang Jih-pao where, in accordance with Mao's comments at the Peitaiho Politburo Conference, he advocated reform of the supply and wage systems. Mao was reportedly so pleased with Chang's "Break Away from the Idea of Bourgeois Right" that he ordered its reproduction in Jen-min Jih-pao and personally wrote an accompanying "editor's note" supporting its assertions.[9]

K'o continued during the Great Leap Forward and afterward as one of Mao's most consistent supporters, and he continued to draw upon Chang's involvement. K'o's support was considered by Mao to be a key factor in his launching of the Great Leap,[10] and throughout the period 1958-63 K'o published actively on ideological issues, often defending the "general line" forwarded in the Leap.[11] Chang's active support of K'o's political activities during this period earned him increasing prominence in the Shanghai Party hierarchy. Chang was first elected as one of 404 members of the Municipal Party Committee in 1958, and in less than one year was elevated to its 81-member Standing Com-

mittee.[12] It was, however, in his earlier-acquired position as head of
the Literary and Art Work Committee of the Municipal Party Committee's Propaganda Department that Chang made his influence felt during
the early 1960s.

In the aftermath of the P'eng Teh-huai affair, China's Propaganda
hierarchy began to divide over many of the very types of policies pushed
by K'o and Chang during the preceding period as well as over the dismissal of P'eng himself. Chang became associated during this period
with a faction of younger officials within the national Propaganda hierarchy including such figures as Yao Wen-yuan, Kuan Feng, Ch'i Pen-
yu, Lin Yu-shih, and Lin Chieh. This group continued to press for
criticisms and reform of "bourgeois" tendencies in literature and scholarship, became embroiled in a number of literary/political controversies
with another group of officials who opposed this continual "class struggle,"
and dissented from P'eng Teh-huai's dismissal and, by implication, from
the line of policy represented by the Great Leap Forward.[13] During
this period, Chang, emulating his superior K'o in defending these policies,
used his position as head of the Shanghai Literary and Art Work Committee to criticize and provoke Party members and others holding dissenting views. Yao Wen-yuan, who had been one of the primary critics
of "bourgeois" tendencies in literature and scholarship, quite naturally
became one of the defenders of this militant literary policy.[14] When
Pa Chin, chief editor of Shanghai's Wen-i Yueh-pao, objected in 1962
to Shanghai Party writers who look everywhere for "mistakes" and
"bring the club down" on the heads of those who disagree with them, he
himself became a target of Yao's attacks.[15] In the ensuing split within
the local Propaganda Department, Chang defended Yao, while Ch'en
Ch'i-wu and Yang Hsi-kuang, deputy directors of the Propaganda Department, reportedly sided with Pa and enlisted the support of the Propaganda Department head, Shih Hsi-min. At one point, deputy director
Ch'en Ch'i-wu declared his intention to bring back writers from rural
villages who had earlier been sent packing as "rightists" by the likes
of Chang and Yao during previous campaigns in Shanghai. This prospect was apparently unacceptable to K'o Ch'ing-shih, who intervened in
the spring of 1963 to dismiss Ch'en Ch'i-wu from the Party, remove
Shih Hsi-min from his post, and to replace Shih with a new Propaganda
Department head, Chang Ch'un-ch'iao.[16]

Upon being promoted to head the Municipal Party Committee's
(MPC) Propaganda Department, Chang quickly became a member of the
highest echelon of Shanghai Party leadership. Only seven months after
his appointment to the Propaganda post in May, Chang was elected in

December 1963 as one of forty-five members of the Third Shanghai Municipal Party Committee.[17] The following February, only two months afterward, he became an alternate member of the Secretariat of the MPC, and by March 1965 he was a full secretary on the MPC's Secretariat.[18] With K'o Ch'ing-shih's support, Chang had come to occupy a political post that proved to be a pivotal one in the intensifying debate over literary and cultural policy.

K'o Ch'ing-shih now had an extremely helpful local Propaganda chief for his efforts to push, along with Mao, for reform of China's dissident intellectuals and Party Propaganda personnel.[19] As part of this effort, Yao Wen-yuan was promoted during this period to chief editorship of both Wen-hui Pao and Chieh-fang Jih-pao.[20] This was also the period during which Chiang Ch'ing first became active in cultural politics, coming to Shanghai at one point to produce her new "revolutionary" operas.[21] But in April 1965, just as this flurry of political activity in the arts was gaining momentum, an unexpected event occurred which was crucial in shaping the subsequent form the Cultural Revolution would take in Shanghai: K'o Ch'ing-shih died while at a Party meeting in Chengtu.[22]

K'o's death in no way quashed the emerging efforts of his like-minded Shanghai colleagues to create further pressure and confrontations over art and literary policy. Yao Wen-yuan's well-known article criticizing Wu Han's play, "The Dismissal of Hai Jui," was still published in Shanghai's Wen-hui Pao in November, precipitating the conflict that would eventually lead to the purges of Teng T'o, Wu Han, Liao Mo-han, P'eng Chen, and other Peking Party figures in the spring of 1966.[23] K'o's death did, however, thrust into top leadership positions two officials who had worked under him for the past decade and who were now asked to administer China's largest city in a highly uncertain and rapidly changing political environment. The first- and second-ranked Shanghai Party members after K'o's death--Ch'en P'ei-hsien and Ts'ao Ti-ch'iu--would split the duties formerly held by K'o. Almost simultaneous with the initial debate over Yao's Wen-hui Pao article on Hai Jui, Ch'en was appointed first Party secretary for the MPC, and Ts'ao, at the Municipal People's Congress held in early December 1965, was elected mayor.[24] The actions of both of these new municipal leaders, who would eventually be purged as local revisionists, were crucial in shaping the course of the Cultural Revolution in Shanghai.

Ts'ao Ti-ch'iu's Political and Organizational Background

Ts'ao's political concerns and actions both before and during the Cultural Revolution, so often contrasted with those of Chang Ch'un-ch'iao, deserve closer analysis. A re-interpretation of Ts'ao's role in Shanghai is essential for a new understanding of Chang's actions. For one who has been portrayed in so many accounts of the Cultural Revolution as a resister of the movement in Shanghai, Ts'ao's previous career in fact bears striking political parallels to those of both K'o Ch'ing-shih and Chang Ch'un-ch'iao. Ts'ao had apparently played a supporting role for K'o Ch'ing-shih in the management of Shanghai's economy analogous to the role played by Chang in propaganda efforts and literary affairs. As early as 1957 Ts'ao, already a vice-mayor and secretary of the MPC, had praised the then-current upsurge in rectification and anti-rightist campaigns, stressing the importance of the downward transfer of high level cadres. Ts'ao underlined the need to fight bureaucracy and the importance of manual labor in transforming world outlook, eliminating the "three great differences," and diffusing expertise.[25] In a speech the following year, moreover, Ts'ao stressed, just as Chang Ch'un-ch'iao had that very year in his article for Jen-min Jih-pao, that the rectification of "bourgeois rightists" was necessary in the protracted struggle to "annihilate" the bourgeoisie.[26]

Ts'ao had apparently been, at least at times, a useful political ally for K'o Ch'ing-shih. But unlike Chang, whose organizational position up to that time led him to concentrate on the political content of ideas expressed in literature and art, Ts'ao was faced with the complex task of putting political concepts successfully to work in industry. While Chang's writings, like Ts'ao's speeches, highlighted the corrosive effects of liberal thinking and nonsocialist economic practices, Ts'ao was additionally responsible for actually implementing the policies advocated--at times fashioning a system for high level cadres to participate regularly in labor and devising means for workers to participate usefully in technological innovation--while at the same time assuring not only that production went unhampered, but that it actually increased. Central to the successful raising of industrial production, Ts'ao asserted in 1964, was the "ideological awakening" of the "human factor" that had proved so important to the success of Shanghai's industry since the Great Leap.[27]

Thus Ts'ao Ti-ch'iu had himself contributed, just as had Chang, to K'o Ch'ing-shih's efforts to support Mao's central policy initiatives in the decade preceding the Cultural Revolution. Shortly after being promoted to mayor, Ts'ao signaled his intentions to continue to forward the policies of his deceased predecessor. Within three months after his official designation as mayor, Ts'ao praised, at worker and peasant conferences in March and April 1966, the accomplishments of the Socialist Education Movement in Shanghai--the implementation of the "mass line" in basic level leadership, the study of Mao-thought, the bringing of politics to the fore in enterprise management, and the creation of "new Communist men." But Ts'ao went beyond these general pronouncements and went to the core of what was later to become known as the Maoist line--a line towards which Ts'ao was eventually accused of being unalterably opposed. He stressed that class struggle did not end with the Socialist Education Movement and that continued ideological revolutionization was a necessity. Far from impeding production, such a campaign would, through ideological revolutionalization, bring "greater, faster, better, and more economical results." Increases in production, however, were not the primary goal; this campaign was essentially "for transforming man and enterprise with the thought of Mao Tse-tung, a profound ideological and revolutionary campaign for promoting proletarian ideas and destroying the bourgeois ones. . . ."[28]

Ts'ao Ti-ch'iu, in effect, reiterated in his first ninety days as mayor a commitment to Mao/K'o policies and slogans that he had exhibited in pronouncements dating back to 1957. Then, just as he was settling into his new office, events in Peking drastically altered the Party organization's political environment. The political infighting following Yao Wen-yuan's criticisms of Peking literary and propaganda circles had resulted in the purge of several prominent Party officials-- among them P'eng Chen, who held positions as mayor and first Party secretary of Peking Municipality. Ts'ao and Ch'en P'ei-hsien shared the same posts in Shanghai. This fact, coupled with the immediately following campaign to root out similar "revisionists" in culture and art--even those within the Party apparatus--must have presented Ts'ao and Ch'en with a highly uncertain and potentially threatening political environment.

III

THE CULTURAL CAMPAIGN
MAY–AUGUST 1966

By mid-1966, Ch'en P'ei-hsien had withdrawn from his only recently acquired position as Shanghai's first Party secretary due to "ill health." It is not clear whether Ch'en's illness was physical or political in nature--Red Guards would later claim that he had faked his illness in order to escape criticism and removal--but it is clear that Ch'en would not play any visible role in Shanghai until December, only weeks before his ouster.[1] Ts'ao Ti-ch'iu thus became both mayor and acting first Party secretary--an organizational position identical to that of the ill-fated P'eng Chen. Perhaps partly as a continuation of his past support for Mao/K'o policies, and perhaps partly conscious of the April demise of his Peking counterpart and of his own political vulnerability, Ts'ao became a vigorous proponent of the Cultural Revolution in its earliest stages.

Ts'ao's June pronouncements indicate his conception of what the Cultural Revolution would mean for Shanghai--a conception that was probably very close at this point to that held by Chang Ch'un-ch'iao and Yao Wen-yuan. According to a statement he released on June 4, "the clearest definition of our policy" is that the main targets of criticism will be those "hypocrites who wave the red flag as a cover for an attack on the red flag." Even if the movement "should turn into an inner-Party struggle, the target will remain the same. . . ."[2] Again, at a well-publicized mass rally on the 10th, Ts'ao gave his clearest pronouncement on what he intended the Cultural Revolution in Shanghai to be:

> The great Cultural Revolution that is now under-
> way will be an exacting test for the Party spirit and the
> revolutionary spirit of every Party organization, every
> individual Party member, and every revolutionary
> cadre. The way you approach the crucial questions
> raised by this movement will reveal whether you really
> believe in socialism or only pretend to believe in it or
> are actually opposed to it, whether you really support

11

Mao Tse-tung's ideas or only pretend to support them or are actually opposed to them.[3]

As for those who are found to be "playing with revisionism," "we will have our means to expose him and completely topple him, no matter how high his official position, and no matter what kind of 'authority' he is."[4]

Students struggling against their university administrations apparently responded enthusiastically to Ts'ao's speech. An organ of what Neale Hunter considered to be a "radical" organization at the Foreign Languages Institute noted that Ts'ao stressed fully three times that the movement was directed against Party authorities leading China back towards capitalism.[5] This same organization quoted Ts'ao in order to criticize the school Party Committee's attempt to orchestrate criticism around a number of "bourgeois academic authorities"--usually professors who had been criticized in earlier anti-rightist campaigns.

At this stage of the Cultural Revolution Chang and Ts'ao probably worked in close cooperation. The targets of the summer campaign were invariably individuals who had been critics of the Party and of K'o's policies--especially of the Propaganda Department--since the Hundred Flowers period. A significant proportion of those earmarked for criticism had been directly engaged in controversies with either Chang or Yao Wen-yuan. Throughout most of the summer, Chang, as Propaganda chief, directed criticism against individuals who had opposed the policies he had carried out as head of the Literary and Art Work Committee over the past decade in Shanghai.[6]

At the June 10 mass meeting which launched this stage of the movement in Shanghai, Ts'ao Ti-ch'iu, with Chang Ch'un-ch'iao in attendance, delivered a militant speech echoing the attacks on "bourgeois rightists" that Chang and Yao Wen-yuan had been making for years.[7] Calling the imminent Cultural Revolution a "life and death struggle with the bourgeoisie," Ts'ao warned that "the historical experience of the dictatorship of the proletariat reminded us that in carrying out counterrevolutionary activities for restoration," the bourgeoisie has resorted to "using a pen to spread vicious ideas in the realm of ideology." This first step--getting a "grip on ideology"--entailed carrying out "anti-Party and antisocialist propaganda in the form of theory, academic discussions on art and literature to lay ideological groundwork and create public opinion for the restoration of the bourgeoisie."[8] Warning that "the representatives of the bourgeoisie both inside and outside the Party are scheming such a conspiracy" and presenting the "anti-Party and antisocialist crimes" of the purged Peking literary bureaucrats as an example, Ts'ao asserted that "similarly cunning people" existed in government, Party, army, and cultural circles within Shanghai.[9] The meeting concluded with a report naming such representatives of the bourgeoisie in Shanghai, and provided the focus for the summer's rectification campaign.[10]

During these summer months the Party Center's work-team policy implemented by Liu Shao-ch'i and Teng Hsiao-p'ing meshed nicely with the local efforts of Ts'ao and Chang to remove long-standing opponents of the Literary and Art Work Committee. Under Liu's orders, Party work teams were dispatched from Peking to universities in the provinces where top school officials were removed and criticism campaigns against them organized.[11]

One of the first school administrators removed and criticized in this fashion was Ho Lu-ting of the Shanghai Music Conservatory--an outspoken resister of the types of literary and art policies forwarded by Chang under K'o Ch'ing-shih's administration. Ho, an outstanding theorist of musical composition, had composed while in Yenan what amounted to the Chinese national anthem, "The East is Red," dedicating the score to Chairman Mao.[12] As early as the 1957 anti-rightist campaign, however, Ho had made enemies within the Propaganda Department by refusing to implement the campaign within his conservatory, arguing that the critics of the Hundred Flowers period had been assured immunity and that these promises had to be kept.[13] During the Hundred Flowers period, in fact, Ho had himself been a critic of the Party, calling for a "democratic system of education" within his music conservatory.[14] During the relatively liberalized period of 1961-62, Ho had continued in this role--decrying the politicization of music, saying that Party policies regard musicians as "music making machines" and deriding the quality of politicized music.[15] As was quite common for such critics of Party cultural policies, Ho's call for liberalization during this period led him into direct conflict with Yao Wen-yuan. After Yao had written, in 1963, an article criticizing the turn-of-the-century French composer Debussy, Ho responded to Yao. Issuing a statement to reporters and writing an article under a pseudonym, Ho reportedly labelled Yao a "bruiser" who "used a club to knock down everything."[16] This history of opposition to the policies of the Propaganda Department's work committees made Ho a prime target in the summer of 1966.[17]

Another targeted intellectual with a background of conflict with the local Propaganda Department was the prominent Futan University historian, Chou Ku-ch'eng. Chou was mentioned as early as 1958 as one of thirty-four Futan University professors who had publicly pledged to reform their thinking in the wake of the previous year's anti-rightist campaign.[18] In 1963 Yao Wen-yuan had criticized Chou's writings on the dialectic, accusing him of neglecting conflict as necessary in processes of change.[19] To this criticism Chou had responded, re-asserting his position that the "spirit of the contemporary age" was not one of various contradictory strains in revolutionary conflict but one of contradictory strains combining into a harmonious whole. Yao's "abstract generalizations," Chou had asserted, simply did not accord with the facts.[20] Even in the earliest stages of the Cultural Revolution, Chou had subtly criticized Yao Wen-yuan. In a Wen-hui Pao forum discussing Wu Han's "Self-Criticism on 'Dismissal of Hai Jui'" in January 1966, Chou declared that more serious historical studies of feudal property relations needed to be completed before a "war of annihilation" is waged against Hai Jui. Wryly criticizing Yao in an elliptical fashion, Chou suggested that more "antagonistic views" (i.e., Yao's criticisms of Wu Han the previous November) were being published at that time because they were popular with the reading public.[21] This history of conflict with Yao and Chang earned Chou the title of "bourgeois revisionist" in the summer 1966 campaign and saw him linked with the already purged national propaganda official, Chou Yang.[22]

Other targeted figures, while sharing this common history of conflict with Chang's Literary and Art Work Committee and with Yao Wenyuan personally, were also tied directly with the purged cultural figures in Peking. Chou Hsin-fang, for example, a well-known Peking opera singer who had been active in the May 4th movement of the 1920s,[23] had a history of collaboration with Wu Han in writing and producing Peking operas. It was perhaps inevitable that Chou would come under attack, since Wu Han, in his preface to the published version of his much-maligned Hai Jui's Dismissal, explicitly acknowledged Chou Hsinfang's influence on his own playwriting.[24] In the early 1960s, Chou himself had written Hai Jui Sends a Memorial to the Throne, the play that Wu Han claimed had inspired his efforts, and had produced a similar opera, Hai Jui Admonishes the Emperor, in 1959.[25] By 1963 his theatrical activities had already drawn the attention of Shanghai cultural officials in the Propaganda Department--his production of Yang Li-ch'u was ordered stopped because of its allegedly reactionary content.[26] Chou was one of the first targets of the summer Shanghai campaign.[27]

Li Chun-min, like Chou Hsin-fang, was also guilty of authoring a play with a theme paralleling that of Wu Han's Hai Jui. His Tu Fu

Returns Home, published in 1962, was criticized along with Chou's two plays.[28] Li, who had in print only half-heartedly concurred with the criticisms of Wu Han (in the same Wen-hui Pao symposium that Chou Ku-ch'eng had used to slyly criticize Yao Wen-yuan[29]), and who had reportedly objected to others that Yao Wen-yuan's characterization of Wu Han was "unfair," was charged with using his position as deputy director and editor-in-chief of the Shanghai Chunghua Book Company to encourage the publication of reactionary literature.[30] Others who were attacked during this summer campaign had similar histories of conflict with the local Propaganda Department, and with Yao Wen-yuan, during the immediately preceding years.[31]

While the Shanghai press energetically prosecuted local opponents of Chang and Yao, it also directed attacks towards national figures. Ch'en Ch'i-t'ung, member of the PLA General Political Department, was criticized for praising the film "Pressgang," a "poisonous weed" that reportedly had a less heavily political style, portraying peasants "realistically"--in other words, not as model heroes but as fallible humans.[32] Ch'en, like the others criticized in Shanghai, had a long history of conflict with prevailing Party cultural policies. He had expressed opposition to the Hundred Flowers policy in 1957, feeling that it encouraged too many "poisonous weeds"--an opinion in direct conflict with Mao's.[33] This opinion had earned him criticism during the ensuing anti-rightist campaign, after which he was sent back to his native Szechwan for "remolding." During the period of ferment in the early 1960s over political themes in plays, Ch'en had, in addition, been disciplined by the Party at least once (1964) for his liberal views.[34] So even the national figures criticized fit into this familiar pattern: individuals who had experienced run-ins with the Party as early as 1957 and who found themselves in opposition to policies forwarded by Chang and Yao on literature and art in the early 1960s became prime targets for criticism.

The efforts of the early part of the Shanghai movement, however, were not directed solely towards criticism of "revisionists"; a whole array of cultural and educational activities were held at the basic level. Rallies and festivals celebrating Mao-thought were held, and study classes and symposia were conducted for students and workers.[35] Middle school students were mobilized for a well-publicized campaign to participate in farm labor in the suburban counties and to develop dramatic presentations of "revolutionary culture" with which to entertain their peasant hosts.[36] Another campaign urged youths, on the basis of Mao-thought, to volunteer for participation in rural labor in Sinkiang.[37]

This period was by no means one in which, as later charged, Ts'ao and other MPC officials had restricted and suppressed the movement or even directed criticism to insignificant figures. It appears rather that during this early phase of the Cultural Revolution, Chang teamed with Ts'ao to criticize and remove individuals who had over the previous decade resisted Chang in his organizational position as head of the Literary and Art Work Committee of the Municipal Propaganda Department-- the organ directly responsible for policing these dissident intellectuals. While Chang came into conflict with these individuals over genuine issues of politics and art, his position in the Work Committee seems decisive in the selection of individual targets of attack.

IV

TS'AO TI-CH'IU AND THE EARLY
RED GUARD MOVEMENT IN SHANGHAI

While Ts'ao had successfully carried out--in apparently close
cooperation with Chang--the summer rectification campaign that marked
the beginning of Shanghai's Cultural Revolution, a novel and ultimately
more complex task would shortly confront him. The student movement
would soon be designated as the central focus for the next months of the
Cultural Revolution. At the Eleventh Plenum in Peking in early August,
Mao criticized Peking Municipal Party officials for suppressing the
student movement with work teams and for prohibiting their activities
in public. Both he and Lin Piao made it clear that Party members were
to be judged on the basis of their attitudes towards the student movement
and towards Mao-thought. In his closing speech at the Plenum, Mao
uttered a phrase that must have rung in the ears of someone in an organizational position similar to P'eng Chen. This utterance is a key one in
understanding Ts'ao Ti-ch'iu's behavior during the Cultural Revolution:

It must by no means be taken for granted that
everything which is written down in our resolutions
will be implemented by all our Party committees
and all our comrades. There will always be some
who are unwilling to do so.[1] [Emphasis added.]

Not surprisingly, immediately after Ts'ao returned from this meeting
in mid-August, the MPC organized a citywide federation of Red Guard
organizations. Originally called the "General Headquarters of Red
Guards from Shanghai Schools and Colleges," this group aimed itself
not at "dragging out" the MPC leaders but at eradicating manifestations
of bourgeois culture and ideology in the city.[2]

Ts'ao actively encouraged this sector of the Red Guard movement
and its aims. At first, most of the public activities were organized by
the MPC. The second half of August was characterized by orderly Red
Guard parades, speeches, and rallies, largely in praise of Mao-thought.[3]

17

Ts'ao spoke at a number of these rallies, where he hammered at a constant theme:

> In making the Great Proletarian Cultural Revolution we must manifest a revolutionary spirit--daring to blaze the trail, to act, to make revolution and to rebel. We must rebel against all those in power who take the capitalist road. We must knock down all the reactionary authorities of the bourgeoisie and the bourgeois royalists. We must oppose all those who repress the revolutionary acts. [4]

With these actions and words Ts'ao was making sure that he complied with the letter of Mao's Eleventh Plenum instructions, thus ensuring his safety from P'eng Chen's fate. The "capitalist roaders" that Ts'ao had in mind, however, were clearly of the sort that had been targeted in the earlier rectification campaign. Ts'ao certainly agreed with his acting Propaganda chief, Yang Hsi-kuang, who was reported to have said, "The Shanghai Municipal Committee scrupulously follows the instructions of Chairman Mao. It is nothing like the Peking Municipal Committee." [5] Subsequent events were to prove that Ts'ao and his fellow MPC secretaries did not consider themselves "capitalist roaders," but legitimate beneficiaries of Mao's authority, and by their strict adherence to central directives they were intent on proving so.

Encouraged by the active support of the MPC, this sector of the Red Guard movement took to the streets to propagate Mao-thought and attack manifestations of bourgeois ideology. Shanghai Red Guards formed themselves into propaganda teams and fanned out into the city: putting up posters, distributing handbills, and giving lectures on Mao-thought on street corners, in parks, at bus stops and inside the buses themselves. [6] They formed official "Mao-thought Propaganda Teams" which were allowed to enter into the Departments of Finance and Culture to search out manifestations of backward ideology in these municipal units. [7] Some of the roving propaganda units took their attack on bourgeois culture in the literal sense and harassed people with Western hairstyles or clothing; removed coats of arms, bas-reliefs of clipper ships, and other symbols of foreign domination from buildings on the Bund; and raided Shanghai's churches, removing decorations and religious objects. [8] The elegant homes of former capitalists in neighborhoods near the Bund were searched for luxury items, weapons, foreign currency, or anything else deemed suspicious, and stores selling luxury items were themselves subjected to layers of wall posters and occasional vandalism.[9] This search touched off a marked change in the goods available in Shanghai shops as well as a consumer rush for less expensive, traditional items of clothing, especially Chinese cotton shoes and plastic footwear. As the public hastened to change its image and avoid Red Guard harassment, others formed long lines at the state-run Discarded Articles Company to rid their homes of books, photos and scrolls from pre-Liberation days by exchanging them for the going bulk price for scrap paper.[10] By the end of September the official Shanghai and foreign media both remarked on the striking changes--in dress, street and store names, selection and price of consumer items--in the Nanking Road shopping district. It had become, as one account described it, an ocean of red banners, gold-lettered posters, and Mao portraits.[11]

Shanghai Red Guard Opposition to the MPC

An increasingly vocal minority of the Red Guards, quite probably made up of those sections of the school population deliberately excluded from active participation in the earlier student movement,[12] had become convinced that their exclusion was part of a deliberate policy by Ts'ao to suppress the student movement and protect himself from criticism. Their disputes with their school administrations in October and November about the release of "black material" purportedly collected on activist students earlier in the movement only reinforced this growing conviction.[13] To them, every call for caution by Ts'ao was an attempt to obstruct the movement, and every word of praise for Mao or the Red Guards was seen as a smoke screen. Ts'ao's attempt to nurture and lead a Red Guard movement in Shanghai was, in their estimation, an attempt to divert the orientation of the attacks away from bourgeois authorities on the MPC--chief of whom was Ts'ao himself.

Ts'ao certainly gave this more vocal sector of the Red Guard movement ample circumstantial evidence to reinforce their suspicions. Soon after his initiation and support of Shanghai's citywide Red Guard federation had stimulated an upsurge in student attacks on university administrations, Ts'ao on August 24 delivered a speech at Futan University, a dissident stronghold. He admonished the students to be less frenzied in their attacks, advising that they not "slap a big label" on a person without enough evidence, and defended himself, saying:

> Some say my August 22 speech was too mild, I do not agree. Put my speech alongside the Sixteen Points. Is it mild by comparison?[14]

The majority of Futan students apparently supported Ts'ao's call for careful, well-documented attacks,[15] but to the dissident minority it was simply the latest in a series of moves to suppress criticism and protect revisionists in the municipal Party organization. As an act of defiance, the dissident groups at Futan that very night staged a raid, over one thousand strong, on the campus of the Shanghai Drama Academy. Their midnight foray met with strong resistance from the drama students, and in the debate and brawl that ensued, the drama students, led by a group of Tibetans, defended themselves handily. The student majority at Futan immediately scheduled a large meeting the following evening (August 26) to "study the 16 points," particularly the injunctions against struggle by violence. Ts'ao, in his second Futan appearance in three days, condemned the "adventurism" of the Futan minority, and suggested that they had "confused two types of contradictions" (Point 6) in struggling against other students. When a wave of wall posters criticized the dissidents for breaking the Sixteen Points, the minority declared that a "reign of white terror" had seized Futan and planned a protest rally in Culture Square. [16]

One of the chief sources of dissident anger was their under-representation on school "cultural revolution committees" which Shanghai colleges had formed in compliance with Point 9 of the Sixteen Points. They claimed that these committees were mere appendages of the school Party committees used to suppress the dissident Red Guards. But their exclusion need not have been deliberate--even if general elections had been held (and they may well have been) according to the Paris Commune model by drawing up a single list of candidates for election, it is doubtful that any of the minority groups in a given school could muster the votes to elect a representative. Ts'ao had apparently tried to soothe Red Guard tempers by declaring that these committees would have to reflect "the concern of the majority for the minority" and that

> some students who have played a most enthusiastic
> role in the Cultural Revolution find they have not been
> elected to these committees. . . . They should not let
> their emotions get the better of them. . . . Making
> revolution is not a question of "If I am elected I will
> join in; if not I will not. . . ."[17]

The dissident reaction to this was straightforward: any committee that excluded them, "the revolutionary left wing," was therefore reactionary and must be "rejected, denounced, and smashed."[18]

During the final two weeks in August the MPC's reaction to the local dissidents was benign but firm. The MPC was careful to neither suppress the Red Guard movement nor deviate from Central directives. The students were not declared "anti-Party" or "antisocialist" for their attacks on the Party hierarchy, nor was their right to rebel challenged. What the MPC did insist upon, however, was that the dissident students change their method of struggle. This was communicated to the students not only through Ts'ao's speeches, but also through the mass media. Immediately following the incident at the Shanghai Drama Institute, the media reported on a number of student groups who held discussions on the Sixteen Points and the need to "struggle by reasoning," as well as the need to learn discipline by emulating the People's Liberation Army (PLA). The Tibetan students at the Drama Institute who had acquitted themselves so well in the brawl were praised as "good students of the PLA" and as "defenders of the Sixteen Points," yet nowhere in the media was there any reference to the actual incidents or any criticism of specific student groups. [19]

The Spiral of Conflict: Peking Red Guards Enter Shanghai

The ranks of Shanghai's dissident Red Guards were swelled near the end of August as student groups from Peking began to arrive on "exchanges of revolutionary experience." These Peking students were convinced that the upper levels of the Party were riddled with revisionists and saw the toppling of these power-holders as the only legitimate aim of the Red Guard movement. There were already indications that they meant to perform this task in Shanghai. It was rumored that earlier in August a Nieh Yuan-tzu wall poster in Peking had attacked Ch'ang Hsi-p'ing, head of the MPC's Education Department, as a "revisionist."[20] Besides Nieh's conviction that Ch'ang Hsi-p'ing was a revisionist--a conviction she was probably communicating to her Peking Red Guard colleagues--there were indications that Chang Ch'un-ch'iao was also meeting with and briefing groups of Red Guards bound for Shanghai.[21] One possible target Chang may have directed the students toward was Yang Hsi-kuang, the acting Propaganda Department head who had sided with Pa Chin against Yao Wen-yuan in the Propaganda Department dispute that led to Chang's promotion to the head of the Department. Thus briefed, no sooner had these initial Peking groups left the welcoming reception held for them by the MPC at the train station than they began a strategy of confrontation with the Party establishment.[22]

Their first act was to apply to the MPC for the equipment they felt was necessary to set up a liaison center. They presented Ma T'ien-shui, MPC secretary and head of the Industry and Communications Department, with demands that they be given a seal of office and broadcasting, press, and propaganda equipment. Since Shanghai's own Red Guard groups were only allotted funds and given access to the MPC's own presses during off-hours, the demands were refused.[23] An immediate demonstration outside the MPC headquarters on August 28, demanding to see Ts'ao Ti-ch'iu and air complaints, received no greater response than heckling by hostile crowds and radio lectures to "learn from the PLA."[24] A Red Guard rally at Culture Square two days later declared "war" against Ts'ao Ti-ch'iu, and subsequently, on September 2, more than one thousand Peking dissidents staged a sit-in at the entrance to the Party offices. After two days of radio and press editorials stressing nonviolence and adherence to the Sixteen Points, combined with continual verbal harassment by hostile Shanghai students and workers, the Peking students stormed the MPC offices.[25] Some reports declare that the students were repulsed while others claim that the Peking dissidents, reinforced by their Shanghai counterparts, broke windows, occupied the building and climbed to the roof, hurling stones into the street.[26]

Whatever the details of the event, the MPC's response was firm, immediate, yet conciliatory, as it was for the earlier "Drama Institute Incident." Ts'ao's speech that evening denounced those who "wage struggle by force and not by reason," (Point 6, Sixteen Points) and "strike down everything and rebel against everyone."[27] But he made pains to stress that the MPC would not retaliate, and ordered that "Shanghai comrades are not to strike back."[28] The propaganda campaign against "struggling by violence" was continued in the media, and a telegram of protest to Mao, drafted by workers at the No. 1 State Cotton Mill, was circulated in leaflet form.[29] The centerpiece of the campaign against violence, however, was a recorded speech by Ts'ao broadcasted over the radio welcoming Red Guards from other localities. In it Ts'ao declared that Red Guards of Peking and Shanghai "were fighting for the same goal" and that good meetings had been held in recent days "to discuss and exchange viewpoints." Further:

> We sincerely hope that debate on various questions and differences of opinions will be carried out in accordance with Premier Chou's instruction and under conditions of improved execution of the Great Proletarian Cultural Revolution. . . . We should not be emotional, nor criticize anyone blindly . . . (we) hope revolutionary students and masses will regard the attack on those persons in power within the Party who are taking the capitalist road as the main target of struggle.[30]

The repeated airing of this magnanimous reproof, firmly based on Central directives, infuriated the dissident Red Guards, who would later refer to the MPC response as a "reign of white terror."[31]

Internal MPC Debates about Dissident Red Guards

Red Guard accounts, based upon notes and transcripts seized during a later occupation of the MPC offices in December, give us a vivid account of the Party leadership's perception of this Red Guard "problem." The MPC was clearly uncertain how to proceed in the face of these unexpected, escalating attacks from below. An agenda for a meeting containing questions for discussion suggests the problems with which the municipal leaders were grappling. First was the question of whether there was any truth to the dissident Red Guard claims:

1. Is the main orientation of the Red Guards correct?

2. Should we first consider who they want to "revolutionize"? If they are bent on bringing everyone down, can we say their main orientation is correct?

3. If they spread simplistic slogans like "Long live the Red Terror" or "If your father was a revolutionary, you are automatically a good fellow", does this affect their main orientation?

Second was the problem of how the MPC should deal with Red Guard attacks:

4. There have been a lot of incidents in the streets, and these have been described in different ways. Are the Red Guards at fault, or is the MPC?

5. Among the students there may be counter-revolutionaries who are out to attack the headquarters of the proletariat. Should we single out this element for severe criticism? Some say if we do so now this will have a bad effect on full mobilization of the masses. Others say it would make the ultimate mobilization all the better. Which is the correct answer?

Then, as a basis for discussion, the following course of action was suggested:

There's too much disorder at the moment. The Red
Guards are doing as they please and demanding total
power. Is that right? We have the dictatorship of the
proletariat. Couldn't it do a bit more dictating and
get some more order around here?[32]

Those who proposed this solution were probably, like Secretary
Yang Shih-fa, outraged and embittered by the attacks of the dissident
wing of the student movement. At one of these September meetings
Yang expressed his opinion that the Red Guards were nothing but "vaga-
bonds," "making trouble out of nothing." He charged that they only
"went sightseeing" and, while acquiring no new experience in revolution,
the only experience they summed up was how to disrupt reception stations
and climb walls.[33] He bitterly complained: "Making trouble out of
nothing, they are called revolutionaries, while performing our duties
we are accused of suppressing revolution."[34] Ts'ao reportedly added to
this uncomplimentary description: "They are interested only in violence.
They want to bring everyone and everything down."[35] Still another,
unnamed, secretary objected that the "class origin" of these dissident
Red Guards was "not good," and that their "social connections are complex." This accounted, he felt, for their violent behavior which must
have, at root, "ulterior motives."[36] The MPC wondered whether it was
correct for these students of questionable class background to "monopo-
lize the right to speak at the expense of cadres, workers, and peasants."[37]
Ts'ao ordered that a phone call be placed to Peking to air these opinions.[38]

The suggestions that the "dictatorship of the proletariat" do a little
more "dictating," however much the MPC may have liked to do so, was
not implemented. It was ultimately rejected in favor of a more cautious
policy--one that could not be accused of suppressing the student movement or abrogating the Sixteen Points. The more enlightened policy was
suggested by the acting head of the Propaganda Department, Yang Hsi-
kuang, who warned, "We must be on the alert. We cannot work on the
principle of anarchy. We cannot tolerate the idea that 'everyone is open
to suspicion.'"[39] His proposition was that "most ordinary people are
not too clear about how the Cultural Revolution should be carried out.
We must give them some guidance in the press. We must publish a few
model cases."[40]

This course of action, coupled with a formal telegram to the Party
Center protesting Peking Red Guard violence and requesting their recall,
were the only real decisions taken on the matter. The press continued
to publish model accounts praising the discipline of PLA troops and the

observance of the Sixteen Points by students. Ts'ao continued to give rousing speeches at official rallies praising the Cultural Revolution and Mao's leadership and willfully continued to ignore the dissident students.[41] The Shanghai mass media remained silent on the dissident students and did not acknowledge that the MPC had enemies.[42] Then in late September, for no apparent reason, the Peking Red Guards were ordered back to the capital. The Red Guards claimed that this move was made in order for them to "work as disciplinary corps" for the National Day festivities,[43] but it is more likely that they were withdrawn in response to the deluge of complaints lodged against their activities by Party leaders in the provinces. This phenomenon was to become the central topic of the approaching Party conference in Peking.[44]

Mao's Self-Clarification: The October Party Work Conference

Mao was apparently taken aback by a series of complaints from provincial Party leaders similar to those lodged by Ts'ao. He immediately asked the municipal and provincial Party leaders assembled there: "Why are you old leaders so frightened of the Red Guards? They haven't beat you up and yet you just won't examine yourselves."[45] He asserted that once you have more contact with them "you realize there is nothing to be afraid of."[46] But regional leaders like Ts'ao did not have such contact:

> You are not clear-headed and dare not to face the Red
> Guards, nor speak the truth to the students; you act
> like officials and big shots. First of all you don't
> dare to see people and then you don't dare to speak.
> You have been making revolution for many decades,
> but the longer you do it the stupider you get.[47]

Mao felt that these mistakes were understandable, as were the criticisms he received, for, after all:

> I myself had not foreseen that as soon as the Peking
> University poster was broadcast, the whole country
> would be thrown into turmoil. Even before the letter
> to the Red Guards had gone out, Red Guards had mobi-
> lized throughout the country, and in one rush they
> swept you off your feet. Since it was I who caused the
> havoc, it is understandable if you have some bitter
> words for me.[48]

However understandable, these mistakes had to be corrected. Mao urged the Party leaders to go back to their provinces and municipalities and "hold good meetings" with the dissident students. "Find a quiet place in Shanghai in which to meet. If the students stir things up, let them."[49] "Defensive attitudes" can be transformed, and Party leaders can take the initiative in these matters; but before Party leaders can educate the students, "the educationist should first be educated."[50] The only way to acquire this education, Mao made clear, was to get actively involved in meetings, debates, and self-criticism sessions with the students. If this goal can be accomplished, Mao declared, "That will be that!"; neither the Red Guards nor Mao himself would want to overthrow them.[51] Mao warned, however, "If when you go back you do things according to the old system, maintaining the status quo, putting yourself in opposition to one group of Red Guards and letting another group hold sway, then I think things cannot change, the situation cannot improve."[52]

Even if Ts'ao had understood clearly the sort of things Mao required of him in his dealings with the students, it is doubtful he would have had a chance to carry them out. Less than two weeks after he returned from the October Work Meeting[53] the problems he was faced with changed dramatically, and events occurred so quickly that Ts'ao scarcely had time to deal with them. Ts'ao would soon be faced with a dissident worker movement for which existing Party directives and Mao's latest instructions on the students left him unprepared. In less than six weeks Ts'ao would no longer be exerting his leadership over events in the city.

V

THE CENTRAL DILEMMA
REVOLUTION AND PRODUCTION

While Chang Ch'un-ch'iao remained in Peking, meeting with Red
Guards and instructing them in the art of "rebellion," Ts'ao Ti-ch'iu
and the MPC had throughout this period their normal responsibilities
to attend to, as well as the added task of coping with the dissident student
movement. Chief among these duties was the maintenance of normal
production in Shanghai's factories. From the outset of the movement,
it was asserted that the Cultural Revolution, as a result of revolution-
izing people's thought, would allow them "to achieve greater, faster,
better and more economical results in all fields of work." Any attempt
to present the Cultural Revolution and the maintenance of production as
incompatible was flatly declared to be "incorrect." If the "proper
arrangements were made," it would be possible to carry out both the
Cultural Revolution and normal production without having them interfere
with each other, while at the same time guaranteeing high quality work. [1]
The "proper arrangements" referred to the establishment of separate
leadership groups for production and ideological work, the prohibition
of outside interference, especially by Red Guards, and the maintenance
of labor discipline and of regular working hours, during which "revolutionary" activities were not to occur. [2]

Dissident Red Guards had, from the beginning, sporadically contra-
vened the Center's directives regarding the Cultural Revolution in the
factories and had attempted to establish workplace liaisons--sometimes
damaging work discipline while often meeting strong resistance from
hostile workers. [3] These Red Guards had also, from the beginning, been
repeatedly warned by the Party Center to desist. [4] No lesser Party
figures than Chou En-lai and Lin Piao gave well-publicized speeches
at Tienanmen on September 15, calling for a clear distinction between
the formation of organizations and full-time political activity in the
schools on the one hand, and the vital tasks of production in farms and
factories on the other. They flatly ordered the Red Guards not to tres-
pass in the factories or on the fields. [5] Ts'ao Ti-ch'iu reinforced the
Center's awareness of the problem when he warned on September 24 that

27

it would be difficult to ensure normal production if these attempted liaisons continued, and he suggested recalling Peking Red Guards and ending the "great exchange of revolutionary experience."[6]

The Red Guards were indeed withdrawn to Peking as the October Work Conference approached, but not as a sign of defeat. While in Peking during October, they were being assiduously educated in the art of approaching workers--they were to meet with them after work hours, and gradually ease themselves into factory routine.[7] Despite the fact that workers were still forbidden to form their own organizations, the Peking Red Guards who returned to Shanghai in early November, now known as "revolutionary rebels," immediately set to work organizing workers into groups affiliated with their own.[8] Their efforts, perhaps aided by Shanghai's growing corps of dissident workers, were unexpectedly successful, for on November 8 the city's first workers' organization--The Shanghai Workers' Revolutionary Rebel General Headquarters (WGHQ)--insisted on an audience with Ts'ao Ti-ch'iu to present him with a list of demands.

Ts'ao was once again confronted with an unexpected and wholly unprecedented situation. As the dissident Red Guards had earlier challenged established Central directives on secret archives and files and on struggling by force, this new workers' organization was, by existing CCRG directives, illegal. Ts'ao had two alternatives: he could learn from the reproof he was given in October and apply Mao's advice to become actively involved in meetings and negotiations with the dissidents, or he could take the safe course--the same one he had taken with the Red Guards--and stick closely to established Central guidelines, hoping to "ride out" the difficulty. Probably with Chou's and Lin's recent statements--stressing the fundamental differences between schools and factories--firmly in mind, Ts'ao opted for the second course. This course of action would lead to a confrontation whose resolution would undermine Ts'ao's leadership.

Workers Enter the Cultural Revolution--The Anting Incident

This new workers' organization--the "Workers' Headquarters" for short--was a federation of small cells of dissident workers from throughout Shanghai. Its origins are not entirely clear, but it seems plausible that the impetus for its formation was the effort at political organizing by the student dissidents and dissident middle-level leadership personnel from the factories--most notably Wang Hung-wen of the

No. 17 Cotton Mill. Apprentice workers and contract laborers appear to have been heavily represented in the organization's ranks.[9] When this body, on November 8, sent representatives to the Kangping Street Secretariat of the MPC, it presented demands that their new organization be recognized, that Ts'ao attend their inauguration rally the next day, and that they be provided with finances, press and propaganda equipment. Perhaps having learned something from his earlier confrontations with dissident students, this time Ts'ao received the demands and considered them for half a day before sending his reply via a member of his staff. Ts'ao's representatives explained that the demands were in direct contradiction with existing CCRG policy and could not possibly be met, and they presented the Sixteen Points, Chou's speeches, and the People's Daily editorials stressing the differences between schools and factories as the basis for the decision.[10] Simultaneous with the twenty-thousand-worker mass rally organized by the WGHQ the next day during working hours, the official media responded with editorials praising the Red Guards, publicizing a PLA campaign to "transform world outlook," and explaining the Center's policy on the Cultural Revolution in the factories.[11] Radio broadcasts took great pains to publicize the People's Daily editorial on "Taking a Firm Hold on Revolution and Stimulating Production":

> . . . grasping only production and neglecting revolution;
> or grasping only revolution and neglecting production,
> both are counter to Mao's policy. . . . Schools may let
> out for revolutionary exchange, but production must
> absolutely not be suspended at factories, mines, trade
> and service units and people's communes.[12]

Ts'ao's response had little effect. The Workers' Headquarters drew up five additional demands at their rally, and when these were rejected, twenty-five hundred of their members commandeered a Peking-bound train and left the city, declaring their intention to inform Mao about Ts'ao's efforts to prevent them from making revolution.[13]

Ts'ao, probably in close telephone contact with CCRG members during these few days, then took what was one of the few decisive actions he made during the Cultural Revolution: he had the train stopped at Anting, a siding just outside the city limits, and sent a delegation of friends and family of the dissident workers to the station to persuade them to return. At the same time, unspecified representatives of the MPC (probably fellow workers who were Party members) explained once again the official Central policy about workers' organizations,

liasons, and making revolution after working hours. As a result, over
half of the twenty-five hundred workers returned to their jobs in the city.
All of this took place on November 10.[14] On either the 10th or 11th,
Ch'en Po-ta sent to Ts'ao Ti-ch'iu a telegram which was to be read to
the remaining one thousand Workers' Headquarters members:

> There are two principles involved here, and the minor
> one must be subordinated to the major one. As workers,
> their main job is to work. Joining in the Revolution is
> only secondary. They must therefore go back to work.
> They can take part in the Revolution outside of working
> hours. They should go back immediately. It is a
> serious matter to disobey Party instructions.[15]

This order, when relayed to the workers, apparently had little effect,
for the workers showed no intention of leaving. They remained there
on the 11th and 12th, necessitating further action on the part of the
CCRG.[16] Chang Ch'un-ch'iao was dispatched to Shanghai on the 12th[17]
and was apparently given authority to bargain with the workers in order
to obtain their promise to return to work, for Chang that very day agreed
to endorse the Workers' Headquarters demands. In return, Chang made
certain to secure a pledge from the workers that production and revolution would indeed be reconciled. The Workers' Headquarters immediately issued a public notice for all of their members who had left their
jobs to "return to their factories and plants, and carry out the Cultural
Revolution there."[18] Chang then called Ch'en Po-ta in Peking to inform
him of his actions, and a series of telephone conferences ensued between
Chang, Ch'en, Ts'ao, and Ch'en P'ei-hsien, head of the East China
Bureau. The local Shanghai leaders apparently argued against recognition and support of the worker dissidents, but the CCRG finally decided
to endorse Chang's actions.[19] The next day Chang attended a meeting
at Culture Square where, with the returned Anting workers in attendance,
he officially signed their demands.[20]

Ts'ao Ti-ch'iu was reportedly furious at Chang for caving in to the
demands. In his view, the dissident workers didn't have a leg to stand
on: they were clearly violating the existing CCRG policy, and no less a
person than the head of the CCRG had backed up Ts'ao's position. But,
Ts'ao exclaimed, "Ch'un-ch'iao," for no apparent reason "signs and
catches us with our pants down!"[21] Not only had Chang undermined
Ts'ao's authority, but he had opened a door that the MPC felt would
make industrial production impossible. Ts'ao was forced, however,
to forget his anger for the time being, because 474 of the workers at

Anting who had agreed to return to work had set out for Peking to protest Ch'en Po-ta's "repressive telegram." Led by a worker named K'eng Chin-chang, their "protest brigade" had reached Soochow and was canvassing there for support. Chang and Ts'ao together hurried to Soochow, where they signed their further demands (Ts'ao, reportedly, with some reluctance) and allowed a handful of delegates to continue to Peking.[22]

The MPC's Arguments against Worker Organizations

Immediately following these events, on November 17, the CCRG issued an ex post facto justification for Chang's actions, where for the first time it was stated that "workers have the right to form all types of Cultural Revolution organizations." Given this right, workers were told to make sure that they refrain from factional struggles and work stoppages, that they undertake no revolutionary "exchanges of experience" during work hours and continue to observe the eight-hour day.[23]

Since this was now official Party policy, the MPC was bound to comply; but in their meetings with Chang Ch'un-ch'iao in the week following the incident, the MPC members voiced their criticism of the way the affair was handled and aired their fears over the possible ramifications of the new policy. First there was a series of objections to the signing of the workers' demands. Ts'ao complained, "I may recognize this organization, but why write 'the East China Bureau and the Shanghai Municipal Committee are fully responsible'?"[24] Others objected that Chang's signing had "gone against the instructions of the Chairman, the Central Committee, and Comrade Ch'en Po-ta." Chang had made a "mistake of principle," he had surrendered not on principles of proletarian dictatorship but of "a bourgeois kind of democracy." Perhaps even worse, he had "thrown away the whole position; he has bartered away principles and sacrificed the well-being of the vast majority for the unreasonable demands of a tiny few," and he had "destroyed Party unity" and "embarrassed" the local Party authorities.[25]

Second was the issue of local reaction to the signing of the dissident worker demands. Wall posters had already appeared in Shanghai criticizing Chang's action as a "sell-out," and one MPC member related that the majority of Shanghai's workers were "obedient" to the MPC. He explained that a good number of the workers felt Chang to be a coward and that he "sells out the interest of the working-class."[26] Chou Pi, from the Industrial Production Committee of the MPC, reported that many people had questioned Chang's and Ts'ao's signing of the demands at Soochow and challenged its compatibility with Mao's thought and the Sixteen Points. They were now clamoring for a "10,000-man meeting" to denounce this manifestation of the "bourgeois reactionary line" in the MPC. Even at this early date, a number of workers were threatening to take "revolutionary action" to "smash the rebel headquarters."[27]

Thirdly, and perhaps most importantly, the MPC had strong reservations about the long-term effect of Chang's actions. The consensus seemed to be that the legalization of worker organizations would make the policy of "revolution and production" unworkable. One MPC member asked Chang: "You granted Shanghai's workers the right to form a Rebel Headquarters, but did you even stop to think what effect this might have on the country as a whole?"[28] Vice-Mayor Sun Chi-wen warned Chang that a small disorder like the current one sets back production 10 percent, but that a big disorder "will affect livelihood to such an extent as to paralyze it." Another vice-mayor warned that these events had already affected production and that things could not go on like this for long: "To be sure, we must be mentally prepared for a big disorder."[29] Liberation Daily editor Ma Ta warned: "Once the Cultural Revolution gets going in the factories, there will be no end to it."[30] Chang rebutted these assertions, arguing that the workers' organizations had not caused the disorders but were the result of them. Besides, he countered, the central issue was not the maintenance of production but leaders' attitudes towards mass organizations.[31]

The CCRG was apparently not as certain as Chang sounded on the issue of workers' organizations. Shortly after Chang returned to Peking on November 25, the Central Committee held an important conference to discuss the problems the Cultural Revolution was creating, or might create, in industry. Ma T'ien-shui, the head of Shanghai's Department of Industry and Communications, attended and soon found that there was a discrepancy between the conceptions of the CCRG and those of regional officials as to how extensive the problems were. On the prompting of the vice-chairman of the State Planning Commission Yu Ch'iu-li, who suggested that the regional leaders "tell things as they really are," Ma called back to Shanghai, stating that a "full scale debate looks unavoidable," and asked that the MPC send him more data on the effects of worker disturbances.[32] Apparently a number of regional leaders agreed with the comment made during an MPC meeting: "All comrades of the CCRG know nothing about mass work. . . . The CCRG indulges in high flown talk and has no idea of the difficulties at the lower level."[33] The outcome of the Central Conference--despite local protests by officials who had to live with the consequences of Central policies--confirmed the principle of allowing workers' organizations, though a document was issued on December 9 warning against the recurrence of such incidents as the one in Shanghai. Problems that arose were to be solved through "consultation in the unit itself," and there should no longer be "departures of large groups" from factories or mines. Only when absolutely necessary could workers send representatives to provincial and municipal level organs, and only as a last resort could they send them to Peking.[34]

The Development of Mass Factionalism and the Paralysis of Municipal Government

Ts'ao Ti-Ch'iu's actions to this date were hardly so repressive as was later claimed. He and other members of the MPC clearly had little sympathy with the dissident factions among students and workers, but in his attempts to maintain some semblance of order and labor discipline, Ts'ao had been very careful to follow CCRG directives to the letter and not to suppress the dissidents. This close adherence to bureaucratic procedures, quite possibly designed to ensure Ts'ao's organizational position by proving that he would carry out every Central directive in its entirety became, ironically, the chief reason for the growing attacks against him. Ts'ao, either unwilling or unable to heed Mao's October advice to "take the initiative" by actively meeting with, negotiating with, and engaging in self-criticism with the dissident organizations, chose instead merely to deal with these groups through his office staff. According to organizational procedures established by existing Party policy on the Cultural Revolution, Ts'ao was thoroughly justified in his actions, and his criticisms of Chang after the Anting incident reveal that he fully believed he was justified. In the eyes of the dissidents, however, Ts'ao's actions only reinforced their growing convictions that he was a thoroughgoing "revisionist." His inaccessibility, insistence on some semblance of order, and reliance on established Party procedures--while perhaps necessary for the normal functioning of industry expected by the Party Center--was a stereotype of the unresponsive bureaucrat, "cut off from the masses." Thus Ts'ao, in following the letter (if not the spirit) of Mao's instructions, came to embody revisionist leadership in the eyes of the dissidents. As CCRG policy shifted quickly beneath Ts'ao's feet, moreover, he appeared increasingly as someone who had resisted Central policies all along. Perhaps realizing that his actions had only succeeded in whipping up opposition to him, Ts'ao completely changed his tactics; but this change, in turn, only fanned the flames of mass factionalism that were eventually to render his leadership totally ineffective.

The "Liberation Daily" Incident and the Polarization of Factions. While Ts'ao and the MPC were preoccupied with industrial problems caused by workers' organizations, the dissident student movement had continued to grow both in numbers and militance. Simultaneous with the Central/provincial conference on production at which Ma T'ien-shui was presenting evidence on the local Shanghai disturbances, Nieh Yuan-tzu arrived in Shanghai on November 20, declaring her intention to expose Shanghai's "revisionist" head of education--Ch'ang Hsi-p'ing--and the alleged roles of Ts'ao Ti-ch'iu and Teng Hsiao-p'ing in shielding him. She immediately delivered, on November 25 (the day Chang Ch'un-ch'iao returned to Peking), a fiery speech at a mass rally in Culture Square, where she called for the unity of all revolutionaries in order to bring down the MPC and the bourgeois line.[35]

Shanghai's largest and most militant student organization--the Revolutionary Committee of Red Guards from Shanghai Schools and Colleges, or "Red Revolutionaries"--felt Nieh's speech to be of such vital importance that they imposed added demands upon the Shanghai Party organ, Liberation Daily (Chieh-fang Jih-pao), whose presses had been used to print the first eight issues of their tabloid Hung-wei Chan-pao. They demanded not only that an unprecedented number of copies--650,000--be printed, but also that the issue, including Nieh's call to bring down the MPC, be distributed by the post office along with the daily edition of Liberation Daily. Both the Party Committee of Liberation Daily and the newspaper distribution office of the Postal Department refused the demands and were backed by the MPC.[36] After staging a 10:00 p.m. raid at the post office on November 29 in an effort to secure a promise to distribute the tabloid, the Red Revolutionaries marched to the Liberation Daily building the next afternoon, occupying the building and preventing the daily issues from being printed.[37]

The actual events of the "Liberation Daily Incident," which lasted over a week, are less important than the sharp political polarization these events catalyzed. Large, hostile crowds, mainly composed of people irritated over the interruption of newspaper deliveries, heckled and threatened the protesters and brutalized propaganda teams outside the building who supported the Red Revolutionaries. The Workers' Headquarters, despite their November 12 agreement not to engage in activities during work hours, sent a contingent of their members to reinforce the student dissidents--an action which incited an attempt by the assembled crowd to storm the building. But perhaps more impor-tantly, informal groups of "Scarlet Guards"--workers sympathetic to the MPC's position--began to circulate through the crowds.[38] This occurrence was the first public appearance of that portion of popular sentiment hostile to the dissidents that had been mentioned by MPC members in the meetings following the Anting Incident. The Scarlets charged that the dissident movement was "anti-Party" and "antisocialist" and that it violated the Sixteen Points and Mao's thought by struggling by force, imposing the will of the minority on the majority, and disrupting production with their "revolutionary" activities--clear abrogations of the most recent CCRG directive.[39]

The polarization of these forces was making serious violence a clear possibility. Until December 5, however, the MPC had taken no action except their normal one in incidents like these--the radio aired examples of the PLA as models of discipline and students of Mao-thought worthy of emulation.[40] The Party secretary of Liberation Daily had reportedly called Yao Wen-yuan in Peking to alert him that the Shanghai Party was "in a state of paralysis."[41] On the 5th, however, probably to avert civil disorders, the MPC broke out of its decision-making paralysis and agreed to sign the dissident demands. While the Rebels had been barricaded in the newspaper building their demands had multiplied. Now the Red Revolutionaries had obtained permission to examine Liberation Daily's files and hear a self-examination from the paper's Party Committee. The Workers' Headquarters had tacked on additional demands of its own: the MPC would be responsible for any incidents arising out of the Liberation Daily events and (with obvious reference to the emerging Scarlets) the MPC had to guarantee that other mass organizations did not interfere with rebel actions.[42]

The MPC, however, was no longer in any position to enforce its agreements. First, postal workers staged a walkout and refused to distribute the objectionable tabloid, making its delivery impossible.[43] Second, the Scarlets, outraged at Ts'ao's "capitulation" (as so many workers had reportedly been at Chang's signing at Anting), printed a tabloid, Revolutionary War Express, denouncing the Rebels as "unresponsible dupes of counterrevolutionary manipulators." "Resistance to them," asserted the paper, was "even more praiseworthy than (to) U.S. imperialism." The Scarlets demanded that Ts'ao repudiate his signature and forbade him to "guarantee" anything on their behalf.[44]

The Rebels, seeing the coincidence of these two events, swore they had been tricked and charged that the MPC was controlling the Scarlets and that it had orchestrated the walkout of postal workers. Disgusted by what they claimed was the "continued suppression" of their paper, the Red Revolutionaries held a mass struggle meeting on December 10 against Yang Hsi-kuang, acting head of the Propaganda Department, in Hongkew Stadium. They demanded and received Ts'ao Ti-ch'iu's signature on an agreement to dismiss Yang and report his "crimes" to the Central Committee.[45] The Workers' Headquarters, similarly feeling that the Scarlet propaganda barrage signaled the MPC's intention to back out of its earlier agreement, demanded and received on the same day Ts'ao's signature on a document which placed responsibility for the Liberation Daily incident on him, declaring that the MPC had followed the bourgeois line and expressing full support for the Workers' Headquarters.[46]

Ts'ao's Abdication and the Development of Anarchy. With Yang Hsi-kuang's purge having obtained the prior approval of East China Bureau Head Ch'en P'ei-hsien, Ts'ao perhaps suddenly realized the serious threat to him posed by the mass organizations.[47] Having tried up to that point to stay close to Central directives in coping with disturbances, Ts'ao was now forced to act upon the demands of the mass organizations. Yet, in doing so he still showed a total unwillingness to take a firm stand. Perhaps trying to please both powerful factions, Ts'ao began, on December 10, to sign any and all demands that were made to his office. In effect, he had abdicated his decision-making responsibility, an action which only further incited the factional struggles that would eventually set off the economic paralysis of the city.

The week following Ts'ao's signing of Rebel demands was marked by intense wall-poster debate, spectacular rallies and demonstrations, and more frequent and more violent clashes between rival groups.[48] The Rebels' chief claim was that the Scarlets were an arm of the MPC; the Scarlets claimed that the Rebels were deliberately sabotaging production by leaving their jobs during the Anting and Liberation Daily incidents.[49] At a mass rally on the afternoon of December 21, the Rebels charged that Ts'ao Ti-ch'iu was behind Yang Hsi-kuang and that above them lurked the revisionist Ch'en P'ei-hsien. They declared their intention to "bombard" the MPC.[50] Two days later, the Scarlet faction held a 100,000-person mass rally in People's Square after working hours--a clear rebuke to the Rebels who left their jobs for their rallies. They attacked Ts'ao Ti-ch'iu and had him sign their own list of demands. They wanted, like the Rebels had, recognition; they forbade Ts'ao to enter into agreements that would bind them, and they demanded that they be granted the right to take "revolutionary action" against anyone who infringes on the "laws of the state" or the "discipline of the Party."[51]

Upon hearing this, the Rebels held another rally on December 25, where they had Ts'ao sign still another document, this time repudiating his signature on the Scarlet demands. The Scarlets, once again enraged at Ts'ao's latest capitulation, declared his speech at the rally "worthless" and charged that he had only signed in order to instigate violence.[52] Violence would indeed follow--and soon--and the local leaders were totally powerless to prevent its occurrence. During this period, Ch'en P'ei-hsien reportedly turned to Liao Cheng-kuo, commander of the local PLA garrison, for help. "Shanghai is now in great turmoil. The Municipal Committee has already been paralyzed. Nobody listens to us. Your armed forces must be ready to take over the administration and to work on behalf of the Municipal Committee. . . ." Liao reportedly refused, placing the MPC effectively out of power weeks before the January Revolution.[53]

Ts'ao and the MPC were little more than spectators as they watched events unfold that would lead to the economic paralysis of the city. After abortive attempts by the two factions to close each others' headquarters two days before, the Scarlets, on the 28th, demonstrated in front of the Kangping Street offices of the East China Bureau to "flush out Ts'ao and settle accounts with him." After an attack by a larger force of Rebels, where eight Scarlets were reportedly killed, the Scarlets set out en masse to protest their treatment in Peking. On either the 30th or the 31st they were intercepted and halted by a Rebel pursuit force at Kunshan, about thirty miles outside Shanghai. Among the conflicting reports of the events at Kunshan, it is possible to find two points of agreement: there was violence, and the Scarlets were defeated and turned back.[54] Ma T'ien-shui, who had traveled to Kunshan to mediate and persuade workers to return to their jobs, was placed on a platform and humiliated by the Scarlets, who declared him to be "interfering with their revolutionary action." This treatment of a municipal official, performed by the Scarlet Guards, an organization that was purportedly a tool of the MPC, was a perplexing event and made even more so by the Workers' Headquarters' claim that they had physically rescued Ma from the struggle session.[55]

The decision to permit workers' organizations, and the violent mass factionalism that followed, had thus succeeded in paralyzing the municipal administration. Members of workers' organizations, despite all previous promises not to do so, roamed freely on masse outside factory gates during work hours. Unable to appease either of the mass factions without infuriating the other and unable to employ the military to restore even a minimum of order, Ts'ao's hands were effectively tied. The stage was set for the economic collapse of the city that would necessitate what would later come to be known as the January Revolution.

VI

THE SOCIOECONOMIC ORIGINS OF "ECONOMISM"

Simultaneous with the incidents at Kangping Street and Kunshan, a complex of events took place that later came to be described as "economism." Factory managers appeared suddenly to give in to workers' demands for travelling funds to go to Peking, and workers left their jobs in unprecedented numbers, creating an economic paralysis to match the political paralysis that had already gripped the city's administration for much of December. The official explanation for these events--forwarded under Chang's leadership early in January-- was that the top leaders in the MPC had, as a last resort, offered material benefits to the workers in order to divert the issues of conflict and sabotage the Cultural Revolution by disrupting production.[1] In most Western accounts this explanation is accepted either in part[2] or in whole,[3] but a closer examination of the situation in Shanghai reveals that many workers needed little enticement to become diverted from political issues. For a large portion of the movement, the Cultural Revolution was a chance, above all, to redress social and economic grievances. Further, the standard mono-causal explanation for "economism" obscures the fact that there were actually several different processes occurring in late December to cause workers to make economic demands and leave the job. Finally, this dominant view strains for evidence that the MPC incited walkouts while ignoring the central and obvious role played by the CCRG and the Workers' Headquarters in touching off their occurrence.

Sources of Popular Discontent

The November warnings of Ts'ao Ti-ch'iu, Ma T'ien-shui, and other municipal officials that the legalization of workers' organizations would bring "chaos" were perhaps based on their experiences in recent years in implementing some basic structural changes in Shanghai's economy. These structural changes, the result of recent Maoist innovations in employment and labor allocation, exacerbated existing inequalities in China's wage and employment structure and heightened cleavages within China's working classes. Since the dissatisfactions and conflicts brought about by these recent strains in the Chinese social structure are central to understanding both the intensity and the structure of political conflict in Shanghai in late December, a brief analysis of these socioeconomic trends is necessary at this point before returning to the narrative of events in the last few days of 1966.

The Worker-Peasant System. The sociological element missing from most accounts of the Cultural Revolution in Shanghai--and which makes explanations of "economism" as purely a product of elite manipulation seem so inadequate--is the systematic dislocation introduced into China's social structure by economic policies pursued by the CCP over the immediately preceding years. The worker-peasant system of labor, originally proposed by Mao in 1962 but only seriously implemented after 1964, proved to be a major source of discontent and considerably swelled the ranks of the Rebels during the Cultural Revolution.[4]

This labor system, designed in part to free more industrial surplus for capital accumulation, aimed to lower wage and welfare expenditures by increasing the proportion of temporary and contract labor[5] in the wage bill and decreasing the proportion of permanent labor. In theory, this shift reduces labor costs in three ways: contract and temporary laborers receive a lower wage, they can be discharged during slack work periods to return to their homes or communes, and they are not eligible for the range of union and welfare benefits accorded to permanent labor. By altering the composition of the labor force in this way, a) the total wage bill is lowered, and b) part of the burden of welfare costs is shifted from the industrial system to the communes responsible for supplying contract labor.

Not only economic benefits were to accrue from this system: several social goals were to be simultaneously served. First, income distribution between city and countryside was to be somewhat equalized. By appropriating a significant share of contract laborer income for year-end distribution, the cash income of the rural production brigade supplying contract labor to industry would be raised. Thus in an aggregate sense, industrial cash income was to be diverted to the rural population. Secondly, the system was to help eliminate the "big difference" between peasants and workers by having commune labor work in factories and urban-industrial labor work in rural areas. Thirdly, it would release experienced, skilled laborers to staff growing inland industries and would allow commune members to gain industrial skills--another part of the elimination of the "big difference" between city and countryside. Finally, the system relied on a special form of commune "self-reliance" to provide for the welfare of the contract workers who did not receive benefits from trade unions, a form of self-reliance that would save costs for the national welfare fund. [6]

The push to implement this worker-peasant system in late 1964 had two effects immediately relevant to the later emergence of "economism" in Shanghai: permanent positions in industry began to be eliminated, with the former occupants of these positions often transferred to rural areas; and temporary and contract laborers began to replace the transferred permanent workers. At the first session of the Fifth Municipal People's Congress in September 1964, then-Deputy Mayor Ts'ao Ti-ch'iu urged that "factories and enterprises must employ fewer workers who are permanent. More workers should be temporary." New employees should be "recruited from the peasants so that latent labor power can be tapped." Figures reported from elsewhere in China indicate that this system had, by 1965, been implemented to at least some degree in over thirty different industries, particularly in textiles, transportation, and other light industry--those industries concentrated in Shanghai. In the city of Chengtu in 1965 alone, a total of 7,800 permanent workers were reportedly discharged from employment and replaced with contract and temporary labor from nearby communes. [8] At one storage and transportation company--an inherently periodic operation particularly suited to a nonpermanent labor force--the number of permanent laborers had been reduced by a number of 800, down to 172 workers. [9] With such a reduction in permanent employment looming as an imminent threat, if not a reality in some industries, it is not at all surprising that permanent workers simultaneously voiced their discontent. This dissatisfaction is indicated by the flurry of articles criticizing local labor unions for "corrosive ideology." Workers were criticized for being overly concerned with material welfare and considering only individual interests, and were accused of ignoring the interests of all of China, "especially [those of] peasants." [10] Other articles pointed out that all types of occupations served the revolution and that only "bourgeois elements" felt that they could choose jobs according to "personal wishes." [11] There were apparently very real fears among parts of China's leadership on the very eve of the Cultural Revolution that these worker sentiments would breed what was cryptically referred to as "trouble."[12] This realization perhaps formed the basis for Ts'ao Ti-ch'iu's balking at the prospect of workers' organizations in Shanghai.

This reduction in positions for permanent laborers affected other sectors of Shanghai's population as well. Apprentices in the midst of training programs found opportunities for full-time employment drying up and were often faced with a choice of either unemployment or a stint of rural labor. When students graduating from middle schools found fewer permanent positions available, technical schools began to be organized to absorb some of them, placing them in higher-paying technical apprenticeship programs and threatening to capture the few existing opportunities for the regular apprentices. Those graduates who could not be placed in technical training programs fed a growing corps of "social youth"--a category of unemployed middle school graduates that posed a growing social problem.[13]

Youth Mobilization System. To help remedy this problem touched off by the recent dislocations in employment structure, these youths began to be mobilized in increasing numbers to travel to the countryside to engage in farm labor. This mobilization program would in turn generate grievances among former students. In the few years preceding 1966, over seventy thousand Shanghai youths reportedly had been transferred to Sinkiang alone.[14] In May 1966, as part of the upsurge of the Cultural Revolution, the Shanghai Municipal Party Committee launched an intensified campaign to mobilize youths to volunteer for labor in Sinkiang. Editorials praised the thousands of Shanghai youths who had gone to Sinkiang in recent years and told youths that it was their duty to go. The purpose was "by no means to look for a job" but "to carry on and develop the great work of the revolutionary predecessors and carry the revolution through to the end."[15] Students were told that the criteria for being a "revolutionary" is whether one will "become one with the peasant masses"--otherwise he is quite likely a counterrevolutionary.[16] Mass student rallies were held to whip up enthusiasm for mobilization, and neighborhood registration drives were launched. Simultaneous news broadcasts reported the successful political careers embarked upon by many of the youth-activists already in Sinkiang.[17] There were very real social and political pressures on these youths to volunteer for frontier labor and, judging by the behavior of many of these youths during the Cultural Revolution, a large proportion were less than happy with their prospects.

Resulting Grievances and Conflicts

These dislocations in Shanghai's employment structure gave rise
to a number of socioeconomic grievances that surfaced in the midst of
the Cultural Revolution. Several sectors of Shanghai's working class
needed no urging from the MPC in late December to forward economic
demands. Cadres interviewed by Neale Hunter at Shanghai's docks in
March 1967 admitted that many workers had complaints about their
wages even before "reactionaries took advantage of these dissatisfactions
to divide the masses."[18] Many of these complaints were incidental in
nature and existed relatively independently of the systemic dislocations
of the previous years--older workers complained, for example, that
when they were switched to lighter work, their wages were regularly
cut by over 35 percent.[19] Other complaints arose due to income differ-
entials between shops within a single factory displaying different skill
and productivity levels, forming the basis for intrafactory factionalism.[20]
Near the end of December, many of these disgruntled workers formed
themselves into an array of small groups--of unskilled laborers, old
workers, young workers, and so on--and deluged management with
economic demands.[21] Other miscellaneous organizations were formed
throughout the city on a trade basis: citywide organizations of bus conductors, cooks, and artists were among other groups that pressed
economic demands in December and January.[22]

In a sense, the above groups only added to the prevailing confusion
near the end of 1966. The largest and most important interest groups
that emerged were those that had grievances stemming directly from
dislocations in employment patterns in previous years. These groups
formed the backbone of the major mass factions whose activities would
paralyze the municipal administration and economy.

Apprentices. In China this group serves a particularly long
training period at depressed wages. In past years their opportunities
for full-time employment had dwindled, and they had seen a rise in the
number of middle school graduates who were occupying new positions
in higher-paying technical traineeships. The differences in pay between
these positions were considerable--many complained of the "injustice"
of a student straight from technical or middle school receiving thirty-
five yuan per month as an apprentice technician, while apprentice
workers earned only eighteen yuan per month for their first three
years.[23] Workers interviewed by K. S. Karol at the Shanghai Diesel
Engine Plant revealed that apprentices were the most active in "revolutionary" activities outside the plant and were more often absent from

their jobs during political disturbances than were other workers.[24]
Apprentices from Shanghai No. 3 Steel Mill reportedly formed their
own organization and demanded travel money to "exchange experiences"
in other areas.[25]

Sent-down Youths. Those students who were fortunate enough to
obtain desirable positions as technical trainees were a privileged minority. Most of the youths squeezed out of the labor market during this
period were sent to perform agricultural labor in frontier and rural
areas during the mobilization campaigns of the period. Soon after the
Cultural Revolution began, these students began to return to Shanghai
and formed organizations to protest their "hard work and low wages"
and their "victimization" by the mobilization program.[26] Countless
small organizations like the "1965 Middle School Graduates" and the
"Anti-Japanese Corps" of a Shanghai Youth League plantation in southern
Anhwei returned to Shanghai and besieged the MPC and its Bureaus of
Labor and Agriculture, often aligning themselves with Rebel factions.[27]
In late December, 116 of these organizations, aligned with the Revolutionary Rebels, staged a sitdown strike lasting over a week at a major
Shanghai intersection. Their earlier petition to the East China Bureau
that they be given permits to remain in their home city and look for
jobs had been refused.[28] Chang Ch'un-ch'iao's repeated efforts in 1967
to persuade these youths to leave Shanghai show that many remained
anyway, and some had even been successful in finding jobs.

Sent-down Permanent Workers and Suburban Peasants. The permanent urban workers who had been "sent-down" to the countryside to
become "worker-peasants" lost their union health and welfare benefits,
took a cut in pay, and were separated from their homes on a long-term
or permanent basis, sometimes without their families moving with them.
It is no wonder that when workers began to form their own mass organizations, those Shanghai workers transferred to rural and inland areas
made a concerted effort to return to the city and recover their permanent, higher-paying jobs, with the many fringe benefits that went with
them. In one case, a single factory that had been moved from Shanghai
to central China during 1965 lost seven hundred of its work force to
return migration in 1966.[29] In other cases, workers who had been
transferred to the suburban counties of Shanghai Municipality agitated
for and received permission to return to their original factories to seek
work.[30] The agitation of these former permanent workers in Shanghai's
suburban communes apparently caused many of their peasant coworkers
to re-evaluate their relative positions in the wage and benefit hierarchy,
because a significant number of peasants from these suburban counties

travelled to the city and themselves agitated for equalization of cash wage payments with those of urban workers. [31]

Contract and Temporary Labor. This increasingly important sector of Shanghai's labor force had perhaps the most serious grievances of all the relatively disadvantaged groups. They quickly realized that while performing the same labor as permanent workers, they received lower wages (only part of which they were allowed to keep), were not covered by union benefits or by the plant welfare fund, were not eligible for bonuses or awards in emulation competitions, and were not allowed to sit in factory committees or take time off work for political study classes. [32] When, in addition, worker agitation began to disrupt production in November, these workers, as part of the very logic of the labor system, were laid off in order to save on costs. [33] They formed a large reservoir of radicalized workers and constituted some of the most active and vocal of Shanghai's mass organizations, virtually all of which were reportedly aligned with the Rebel camp. [34] They called for the abolition of the "corrupt" system of contract labor, demanded that they be able to keep a higher percentage of their wages, and those who were laid off agitated for reinstatement and back wages. [35]

Permanent Workers. Not only were there very real socioeconomic bases for the widespread "economism" of the workers' movement in Shanghai, but there were also similar reasons for permanent workers' violent opposition to the dissident Rebel movement swelled by the ranks of the disadvantaged sectors of Shanghai's working class. These reasons highlight that it was possible, contrary to that which is asserted in most accounts, that permanent workers acted spontaneously and independently of MPC direction. Just as for the dissident workers, the behavior of privileged permanent workers was based in no small measure on the network of economic relations in which they worked and lived. The trends of the previous few years had clearly threatened the positions of Shanghai's permanent workers, as they were gradually being replaced with contract and temporary labor. If this trend, or the perceived threat posed by it, was not enough in itself to cause resentment of the disadvantaged sectors of the labor force, then the agitation by these disadvantaged groups in November and December was. Permanent workers had a very real stake in the maintenance of production-- their bonuses and in many cases their wages (if tied to piece rates) were dependent upon the continuing productivity of the firm in which they worked. [36] When disadvantaged groups disrupted production by leaving their positions in the factory, permanent workers' incomes were directly--and perhaps drastically--reduced. Quite naturally, the

Scarlet Guards--who were characterized by opposing factions all along as being tied with the labor unions of the permanent workers--chastised the dissident factions for abrogating the Sixteen Points by leaving their production posts, and were indignant over MPC capitulations to their demands. [37]

Social Conditions in Shanghai--December

Not only were there genuine socioeconomic foundations for spontaneous formation of interest groups and the appearance of "economism," but social conditions deteriorated in the city during the course of the Cultural Revolution, contributing independently to the economic collapse so often laid to the machinations of MPC officials.

Massive Population Influx. The flow of returned students, workers, and Red Guard liaisons into the city greatly taxed the city's transportation system and food and commodity supplies. Red Guards on "revolutionary exchanges" alone numbered over one million during the fall of 1966--and some estimates put the number as high as five million. [38] To handle this massive influx, the MPC had set up over fifteen hundred reception centers and staffed them with over 150 thousand workers. When the reception workers themselves began to participate in "revolutionary exchanges" in December, this supportive network of reception centers deteriorated. [39] To this influx of politically or economically motivated groups must be added a considerable flow of tourists from other parts of China taking advantage of the relative freedom of movement of the period. One Japanese visitor to Shanghai during these weeks, for example, reported that an amiable group of students from Fukien requested that he take their picture--they had just come to take in the sights. [40] This visitor and others reported that the streets were literally packed with people (many of whom seemed to be from the countryside) and vehicles, making a trip to the central city a several-hour affair. [41]

Food, Commodity Shortages and Increased Unemployment. Several factors contributed to the creation of the food and commodity shortages. First was the abnormally swollen population of the city. Second, though no less important, were the cutbacks in vegetable supplies to the city due to the disruption caused by struggles over year-end distribution in Shanghai's rural counties. [42] Further commodity shortages resulted from the transport overload (particularly railroads) caused by student exchanges of experience. [43] The commodities that were still available became more difficult to obtain when the city's largest department stores held shortened and irregular hours due to dissident activity in their staffs.[44] These shortages were even more acutely felt by the large numbers of temporary and contract workers who, after being laid off because of a "general reduction" in production, remained in the city and pressed for reinstatement and back wages.[45]

Trigger Incidents for Economic Paralysis: December 26-31

With the socioeconomic origins of "economistic" behavior among Shanghai's working population briefly outlined, and with the deteriorating economic conditions of the city underscored, we are now in a position to offer an alternative explanation of the events at the very end of 1966. The combination of widespread agitation for economic demands, deteriorating economic conditions, and factional violence that characterized Shanghai in late December set the stage for complete collapse of the city's economic life. There occurred within this six-day period a series of trigger incidents, setting off a complex of events resulting in the paralysis of Shanghai's economy. In themselves, these incidents were more than sufficient to touch off this massive wave of "economism," making it unnecessary to assert any plot by MPC authorities to create confusion and preserve their power.

CCRG Decision of December 26. On the 26th of December, Chiang Ch'ing met with a delegation of temporary and contract workers in Peking and endorsed their demands while denouncing the Ministry of Labor and Liu Shao-ch'i for supporting the "corrupt" contract labor system.[46] On the same day, People's Daily published an editorial on "Revolution and Production"--a revised version of a ten-point regulation released earlier that month in draft form--that was an attempt by the CCRG to quell the labor disturbances touched off by their decision to legitimize worker organizations.

This directive, more than any other single event, triggered the incidence of "economism" in Shanghai. It attempted to quell the disruptions caused by agitating temporary and contract workers by giving them back their jobs and getting them off the streets, while at the same time it tried to defuse interfactional violence by declaring an all-out attack on revisionists in factory management.[47] While thus directing factional anger at factory level management, this editorial directed the managers to pay back wages that had accrued while the workers were laid off and authorized them to use plant funds to do so.[48] Here the CCRG is itself performing the crime (of suddenly authorizing payments) attributed to the Shanghai MPC in most secondary accounts. The Workers' Headquarters, closely associated with the temporary and contract laborer movement and quick to press its advantage, presented the MPC on the very next day with a list of demands concerning laid-off workers along the lines of the People's Daily editorial. The MPC, true to form, complied with the Center's policy and signed the demands, [49] leaving Shanghai's industrial managers with access to funds and facing a Peking-encouraged onslaught of worker criticism and economic demands.

General Upsurge of Economic Demands. As temporary and contract workers returned to their former factories to receive their due back wages, other workers, in line with the call to "bombard" the managers, did so with economic demands of their own. [50] The demands ranged from supplemental wages and building up the welfare fund to improving the factory housing project. [51] In many places of work, dozens of small organizations formed spontaneously to press their demands all at once. [52] When peasants and former industrial workers in Shanghai's rural counties heard about the luck of the temporary workers, they too formed their own organizations and travelled to the city to press their wage demands. [53]

The Scarlet Exodus and General Strike. On the day after the Workers' Headquarters agreement and the beginning of the upsurge of wage demands, the Scarlet Guards, badly beaten in a battle in front of the East China Bureau offices on Kangping Street, began en masse to make demands for travelling funds to go to Peking. [54] The issue at this point is whether or not managers, as asserted in later official versions, enticed workers to leave the plant with travelling funds, or whether they were merely unable to resist worker demands. Canton Red Guard Dai Hsiao-ai revealed that student activists regularly and successfully intimidated administrative personnel for travelling funds. [55] The scenes Dai Hsiao-ai describes may pale by comparison with what Shanghai's managers were confronted with on the 28th and 29th. Large groups of angry workers, fresh from a violent and (if we are to believe the descriptions) bloody defeat, possibly still armed with clubs and stones, were probably in no mood to negotiate for travelling funds. Official versions in later press editorials insisted that the initiative lay with the managers (at the prompting of MPC officials), but accounts by workers from individual factories reprinted in these same newspapers often revealed that the managers' shortcomings were that, when confronted, they gave "the green signal" instead of "conducting ideological work among the worker comrades."[56] If this is the case, managers can be accused, at worst, of cowardice, for the existing information indicates that even at the basic level managers did not go out of their way to offer travelling funds.

Simultaneous with the Scarlet demands for travelling funds, the organization's leadership voted to protest Rebel violence and MPC intransigence by calling a general strike of its 800 thousand claimed worker-members. [57] Again, the official accounts assert that the Scarlet walkout, since the Scarlets were allegedly an arm of the MPC, was initiated and coordinated by a "small handful" in the Party leadership. A series of "confessions" by former Scarlet Guards, however, later published to buttress official claims, reveal only that the strike was coordinated by telephone from the Scarlet offices. [58]

The Effects of Economism

A large number of Shanghai's industrial managers appeared, in the midst of dispensing centrally sanctioned back wages to nonpermanent workers, to have failed to discriminate between nonpermanent and other workers when hit with an overwhelming series of economic demands in the last few days of December. Still, this act of dispensing funds to workers for whom they were not intended contributed little to Shanghai's economic collapse; it was merely part of a larger process of industrial breakdown. Dispensing funds to Scarlets made little difference in "luring" them to leave their jobs, since the Scarlets had already called a general strike of their entire membership. The distribution of these funds to other worker groups, moreover, came only after these groups had mobilized, halted work, and agitated for their fair share. In retrospect, the act of dispensing funds to workers was the result, not the cause, of the process of industrial breakdown initiated by the CCRG decision to pay nonpermanent workers their back wages, and it was exacerbated by the peripherally related Scarlet general strike.

With the huge Scarlet contingent absent from work, thousands of Rebels fighting a pitched battle at Kunshan,[59] countless other workers disrupting production by agitating for material benefits, and with intimidated managers releasing huge sums of money to meet their demands, Shanghai's economy came apart at the seams. The funds drawn out of Shanghai's banks caused a "big drain" on state finances and "disrupted the commodity supply system."[60] Rumors spread confusion among the public, resulting in rushes in buying daily necessities and in runs on Shanghai's Municipal People's Bank.[61] A walkout by railway workers on the morning of the 30th coupled with a break in the railway lines at Kunshan (caused by the violence there) completely paralyzed rail transportation linking Shanghai with Nanking and Hangchow.[62] Walkouts, factionalism, and agitation for wages at the docks caused "serious" shipping delays in the harbor, touching off official foreign complaints to Peking.[63] The city's electricity and water supplies were interrupted sporadically as labor unrest and shortages of coal fuel (caused by harbor disruptions) occurred.[64] Industrial production fell off sharply for the same reasons (and additionally because of raw material shortages),[65] and medical services in Shanghai's hospitals were similarly jeopardized.[66] The CCRG's policy of the past six weeks, coupled with a wholly unexpected wave of militance by the relatively disadvantaged sectors of Chinese society, had brought about the economic and political collapse of Shanghai.

VII

CHANG CH'UN-CH'IAO AND
THE JANUARY REVOLUTION

The policies on workers' organizations forwarded by the Cultural Revolution Group in Peking had led, by the first days of 1967, to the chaotic conditions feared by so many regional Party officials, including Ts'ao Ti-ch'iu. Contrary to the efforts of Chang Ch'un-ch'iao and his politically like-minded colleagues, workers did not mobilize simply to criticize "revisionist" leadership and manifestations of bureaucracy. Distinct subgroups within Shanghai's working population formulated their own definitions of "revisionism" according to the real socio-economic grievances they held. Instead of political pressure by an undifferentiated mass--the "people"--upon municipal elites to transform authoritarian administrative practices, a complex array of class-related conflicts and tensions appeared. Contract laborers attacked the labor system under which they were employed, "sent-down" students and workers protested their semivoluntary migration, apprentices rebelled against their meager wages and declining prospects, and former permanent workers tried to reverse their decline in material status. As these groups mobilized to forward their own demands, per-manent workers, threatened by these demands and their associated developments, mobilized to oppose these new workers' organizations. The resulting cleavage led not only to mass factionalism and violence but also to conflicting demands upon municipal authorities. Any MPC action would thus only further incite violence by one mass faction--an unmanageable situation leading ultimately to the administrative and economic collapse of the city.

Cultural Revolution policies, based on the premise that there was no antagonism between production and "revolution," were in danger of being totally discredited by the unexpectedly independent mass action of Shanghai's population. Order and production had to be restored in Shanghai for the Cultural Revolution to continue. Chang Ch'un-ch'iao was dispatched to Shanghai in early January, probably charged by his CCRG colleagues in Peking with the task of restoring order while not sacrificing the political principles whose application had helped spawn

51

industrial breakdown. The ensuing January Revolution was thus not a power seizure by workers' organizations of municipal administration from a recalcitrant group of Party officials but an effort organized by Chang Ch'un-ch'iao to bring mass political action under control and to restore the normal operation of Shanghai's economy.

Chang himself would later be quite explicit about his reasons for returning to Shanghai:

> When we started to seize power, we did not think about using the two words of "power seizure," and there was no such term as "January Revolution" . . . .
>
> We saw personally that the factories stopped operation, the wharves were paralyzed, every day foreign vessels arrived in the Shanghai harbor but could not discharge or load cargo. The imperialists made use of these incidents in their attacks and vilification and broadcast to the world that the Shanghai stevedores went on strike.[1]

Chang related that he planned first to seize control of the "key departments" in order to "ensure people's lives and property against destruction." It was, however, unnecessary to seize power from the MPC and the Municipal People's Council, Chang related, for--probably with reference to Central Party sanctions for his action, the de facto power vacuum in the municipal administration, and the PLA support he was guaranteed--"as a matter of fact, the power of these two organs was already in our hands."[2]

Given this de facto power, Chang's task was twofold: he first had to establish control over key economic and administrative units through the authority he enjoyed over the PLA, Public Security, and key rebel groups--most notably the Workers' Headquarters--thus providing the institutional framework for restoration of production. Chang related, with reference to this first task, that he "decided to take over the key departments: wharves, railway stations, water works, power plants, radio stations, post office and banks" while he "mobilized troops, students and Rebels of some factories and the railway bureau to support us."[3]

The second task--and the one that proved infinitely more difficult-- was to unite warring factions behind his attempt to restore order and production. To achieve this second goal Chang would employ the propaganda skills he had sharpened throughout his Party career. Chang decisively used his control over Shanghai's official media to define and redefine what were deviations, to threaten practitioners of these newly defined deviations, and to actively take the initiative in raising new issues and squelching others. As if to underline the nature of this "revolution," Chang would later admit that this course of action "was not for seizing power on behalf of a certain faction but for our class interests, for the honor of our motherland, for our socialist economy. . . ." The term "power seizure" did not come to characterize these events until later when it "was proposed by Chairman Mao."[4]

Stage One--Establishing a Rationale for Action

By the first day of 1967, with Shanghai in total administrative and economic collapse, and with all major factions harboring animosities toward the municipal leadership, it was probably evident to the CCRG membership that the local officials--who had exercised no effective control over events in the city since late November--had to be removed before order could be restored. The top local officials were rendered without authority because they symbolized revisionist leadership to virtually all major factions in Shanghai--a fact which would have made restoration of order extremely difficult for them. Even if the MPC were able to restore order, however, its doing so would vindicate its earlier stand against workers' organizations and discredit CCRG policies. So for at least two reasons--expedience and politics--the CCRG could not allow the top local leaders to use troops to attempt to restore order.

Instead these local officials would be used by Chang and the CCRG in their initial efforts to mobilize support behind Chang's own attempt at quelling the disorders. On January 1, at the very depths of Shanghai's economic and administrative collapse, Chang and the CCRG began to make the initial moves in their effort to restore order in Shanghai in a manner that would benefit them politically.

The initial act in this strategy was to use the organizational connections built up over the years by Chang and Yao Wen-yuan in the Shanghai Propaganda hierarchy in order to gain control over the local media. The first step that the CCRG undertook to do so was on January 1, when they received a rebel delegation from Wen-hui Pao and granted them permission to "seize power" in the newspaper.[5] Upon the delegation's return on the 3rd, the faction "seized power" in the paper by merely voting to declare themselves in control and printing an edition the next day denouncing Wen-hui Pao's history of anti-Party activities.[6]

Chang immediately flew to Shanghai on January 4 and consulted with the
paper's staff, working on the details of and ensuring rebel support for
the propaganda campaign he would launch the next day.[7]

The opening editorial, supported by a broad coalition of rebel
groups, declared that a "deeper and broader stage" of the movement
had arrived. Attacks in the future should be directed only at a "small
handful" of people within the Shanghai Party. This small group in the
local leadership had tried to resist the CCRG policy of "grasping revolution and promoting production": first by using "production" as an excuse
to suppress the revolution, then by inciting the Scarlets to sabotage
production. They did all of this to sabotage the Cultural Revolution.
These reactionary elements, the editorial declared, must be "dragged
out."[8]

After placing the blame for disruptions squarely upon the MPC,
the editorial moved on to urge workers to return to their jobs. The
editorial declared that workers must now "take firm hold of the revolution and promote production"--this is the policy of Mao and the CCRG.
Workers who desert their production posts are allowing themselves to
be incited by the "reactionary handful." They should exhibit their "sense
of revolutionary responsibility," "stop being deceived and return to your
production posts."[9] Since they were deceived by this handful--upon whom
all responsibility for this incident rested--workers need fear no reprisals
for their desertion.[10] This propaganda strategy had three interrelated
aims: by making scapegoats of the already-discredited and powerless
municipal leadership, Chang sought a) to direct criticism away from
basic level cadres so necessary for the functioning of Shanghai's economy; b) to defuse interfactional disputes by directing attention to a
common, symbolic enemy; and c) to provide a basis for support by the
broadest possible number of groups by excusing workers for being
"misled" by these former leaders.

While the issues in this anarchic first week of January were being
redefined in such a manner that the most effective revolutionary act by
which a worker could combat "the bourgeois line" of the handful of leaders
was now simply to return to work, the handful of municipal leaders themselves were to be exposed and vilified. In a carefully planned and
executed mass rally in People's Square on January 6, complete with
closed circuit television coverage at eighty movie theaters, twenty-seven
college campuses, a variety of hotels and the ten rural counties, Ts'ao
Ti-ch'iu, Ch'en P'ei-hsien, Secretary of Industry Ma T'ien-shui, temporary Propaganda Head Yang Hsi-kuang, and East China Bureau

Secretary Wei Wen-po were led dejectedly onto the stage and accused of crimes ranging from moral degeneracy to high treason. Ts'ao and Ch'en, in particular, were singled out for a long history of allegedly consistent opposition to Mao's policies and to the Cultural Revolution. After confessing their crimes, Ts'ao was ceremoniously stripped of his position as mayor, while Ch'en was required to remain at his East China Bureau post, where he would be "responsible for any disturbances."[11]

Since these leaders had not visibly exercised effective control over events in Shanghai since the end of November, the rally of January 6 was important more for its dramatic effect than for the actual political changes it marked. As the very first step in the restoration of order and production, it presaged what would be the cornerstone of Chang's propaganda efforts during the balance of the Cultural Revolution in Shanghai.

Even though humiliated in such a fashion, these leaders played an important symbolic role in propaganda efforts aimed at restructuring Shanghai's political and economic life. With the "enemy" clearly identified, future undesirable tendencies on the part of workers were to be projected upon this "small handful" and identified as "bourgeois" tendencies that had to be combatted. An intense media campaign was launched immediately to drive home these points. Workers and students who "struggle by force" and among themselves do not realize that the handful of former municipal leaders "exercises control from behind the scenes." The media exhorted that "we should guard against their tricks."[12] If workers were to shift their attention to the "economic struggle" by "putting money in command instead of politics," they would certainly "fall prey to the tricks of the class enemy."[13] In this oblique way--by criticizing the former leadership for inspiring those tendencies Chang sought to eliminate in workers--two political purposes were served. First, those tendencies in workers that were negatively valued-- violence, economic demands, and leaving jobs--were clearly and forcefully communicated as such by identifying them with the purposes of this scheming "handful." Second, and no less important, was the constant theme that workers who "share a common goal" should "unite as one" and "repudiate the bourgeois reactionary line" of the handful of leaders persisting in it.[14] This strategy served the dual purpose of eliminating factionalism and taking heat off of besieged basic level cadres by funneling factional energies towards this inaccessible "handful" who, throughout the period, would serve as a symbol of "revisionism" for the factions to attack.[15]

As had happened so many times before, these events in Shanghai would subsequently be officially approved after-the-fact by Central directives. On January 11, a directive was issued echoing the points that had been made in the Shanghai propaganda campaign since January 4: workers were to resist "corrosion" by material benefits and not be "hoodwinked" by a small handful of revisionist leaders.[16] Further, as if confirming that these events in Shanghai were primarily for the purpose of restoring order, the "Message of Greetings" by the CCP to the Shanghai rebels congratulated them for promoting unity, "grasping revolution and stimulating production," and "upholding the dictatorship of the proletariat."[17]

Stage Two--Strike-Breaking and Political Organizing

Simultaneous with this media effort, Chang, immediately upon returning to Shanghai with Yao Wen-yuan on January 6,[18] plunged into a flurry of organizing activity that would consume him for weeks. From his "joint conference" Chang kept in close touch with the newspaper offices through regular conferences and telephone conversations and met with anywhere from forty to a hundred representatives from mass organizations each day.[19] Chang was coordinating a massive effort to restore Shanghai's economy and civil order while simultaneously enlisting the support of various mass organizations for that effort.

The first product of this activity was the January 9 "Urgent Notice" to the Shanghai people. Chang was able to obtain the support of a broad coalition of mass organizations for a ten-point proposal outlining Chang's strategy for delivering the city from its present condition. Workers were ordered to stay at their workposts and return from "exchanges of experience." Circulating funds (except for normal wage and production expenditures) were frozen, effectively cutting off the money flow that had stimulated the rush of money-related worker demands. The issues of wages and material benefits that had consumed so many workers in the past weeks were officially removed from the revolutionary agenda; these issues "shifted the orientation of the struggle" and were to be postponed "until a later stage in the movement." Any groups that had seized and occupied houses and public buildings must evacuate them or suffer the consequences dispensed by public security forces. The same fate would befall anyone who "sabotaged" production.[20]

These provisions were to be enforced through a two-pronged organizational strategy aimed simultaneously at developing a network for mobilizing and coordinating the activities of the disparate interest groups and at building up a supportive armed force capable of enforcing Chang's administrative decrees. To achieve this first aim--of mobilizing and coordinating mass activities--Chang organized a central command post with fifty representatives from a number of Shanghai's major rebel factions. This anti-economism "Front-line Command for Grasping Revolution and Promoting Production" was responsible for mobilizing the membership of the represented mass organizations to help restore Shanghai's economy.[21] To support these organizational activities and achieve the second aim of the strategy, Chang oversaw the formation of a PLA "Military Control Commission" that was to assist "power seizures" in individual production and administrative units and train a growing public security force.[22]

The implementation of this strategy began the week after the dramatic January 6 mass rally. PLA detachments were posted at banks and other important buildings, took control of the radio station, occupied the airfield, and assisted in a general tightening of public security throughout the city.[23] The "anti-economism command post" simultaneously formed members of workers' organizations into teams that worked double shifts in an effort to fill in for missing coworkers.[24] Members of student Red Guard organizations were placed in strikebreaking teams that filled absented places in unskilled jobs--particularly at the docks and in railroad stations--and organized propaganda teams to convince striking workers to return.[25] PLA units from the Shanghai Garrison and the East China Fleet performed a similar role at the docks and at railroad freight terminals.[26] These teams first converged on the crucial docks and railroads, working to restore normal schedules while putting up posters and distributing leaflets urging workers to return to their jobs and repay the back wages that had been paid to them weeks earlier.[27] Where possible, the various rebel factions at a workplace formed into a "revolutionary rebel committee" which would take over the tasks performed by the "task force" after it left.[28] Outside Shanghai's workplaces, propaganda vans equipped with loudspeakers circulated through the streets, and a countless array of parades, mass rallies and forums were held, all publicizing the current effort to "fight economism" by returning to work.[29] Absent workers, realizing that their strike was being effectively broken, gradually returned to work. By the middle of January reports began to trickle in of individual units that had restored production to almost normal levels.[30]

The Deterioration of Chang's Mass Support. During this second stage of Chang's efforts to restore order and salvage the Cultural Revolution in Shanghai, the relatively broad support he had briefly enjoyed as a result of the dramatic, skillfully stage-managed mass rally of January 6 began to deteriorate. The same organizational efforts through which Chang hoped to mobilize mass support and funnel it into nondestructive activities began to alienate a significant portion of the groups that had formed the "Rebel" camp late in 1966.

Some secondary accounts have attributed this deterioration of Chang's mass support to his abandonment of the Commune in late February.[31] This process of deterioration actually began as early as the middle of January--a process to which several factors contributed. Probably most important was the fact that Chang's policies--to return back wages and shelve economic grievances--directly conflicted with the expressed interests of many groups in the rebel faction. Apprentices and nonpermanent laborers had forwarded economic grievances and had been very active in the dissident movement. Since Chang had returned to Shanghai they had been asked to give up the prizes they had won in earlier struggles. A second factor was Chang's use of the PLA to take over banks, airports, radio stations, and other key economic and administrative units. When doing so the troops often met with opposition from rebel groups other than the Workers' Headquarters who had already seized nominal control of these units. This tactic was viewed by the rebel groups involved as "suppression." Thirdly, it is likely that certain factions such as Wang Hung-wen's Workers' Headquarters were more heavily represented in Chang's organizational network--for example, in the "anti-economism command post"--than were other major organizations. When detachments from the Workers' Headquarters moved into units to "seize power" as part of their strategy of restoring order, they often conflicted with other rebel groups already established in those units. These three factors combined into a pattern that led many rebel organizations to question whether Chang himself was a "revisionist" and fueled renewed factional infighting--this time within the old "Rebel" camp over the issue of Chang Ch'un-ch'iao's moves to assert control over the chaotic mass movement.

The nascent resistance to these organizational thrusts was compounded by Chang's opposition to independent attempts by mass organizations to seize administrative power from the MPC and set up a new form of municipal administration. During the period that Chang coordinated rebel activities from his office there were three separate attempts to "seize power" from the MPC. Chang squelched each one, persuading the organizations involved that the action was premature and preventing the press and radio--firmly under his influence--from giving the actions publicity.[32] Chang had a different plan for the "power seizure" in mind than did these mass organizations and was carrying it out through the combined activities of the "command post," the PLA, and resurgent public security forces. Some groups began during this period to complain of persecution at the hands of these organs and the Workers' Headquarters.[33] Others, like the Red Flag Army, a large organization of demobilized soldiers, violently opposed the PLA take-overs at the airport and radio stations and had even carried out raids on army posts, public security bureaus and the Liberation Daily.[34] A growing corps of rebel groups were becoming highly hostile towards Chang because he was a former MPC official and, to their minds, was increasingly acting as one.

It is not surprising that when Chang sent messengers to all the major rebel organizations in Shanghai as he was preparing to found the Commune that some of the most powerful refused to take part. Chief among those who refused were Keng Chin-chang's Second Regiment, a reportedly 520-thousand-strong workers' organization closely aligned with thirteen smaller groups;[35] the Workers' Third Army, a several-hundred-thousand-strong organization that had earlier broken away from the Workers' Headquarters on January 7; the Red Flag Army, a large organization of demobilized soldiers; and two student groups, Ching-kangshan and the Red Revolutionaries, the latter being the largest and most powerful student group in Shanghai.[36]

As Chang's efforts to restore order and assert control met with growing resistance, he was forced increasingly to rely upon military support to carry out his plans. A self-reinforcing spiral of declining popular support and increasing use of coercion characterized the last half of January and early February. Through the support of the PLA, Central Party approval, and the substantial Workers' Headquarters organization, Chang exercised de facto political power, but the broad mass support so vital for the implementation of his plans to restore order to Shanghai's Cultural Revolution continued to elude him.

As the relations between Chang and the groups opposed to him deteriorated, Keng Chin-chang combined forty-eight organizations into a united opposition--the "Shanghai Revolutionary Committee of Broad Unity." He promptly launched a furious propaganda campaign to head off the formation of Chang's Commune and led a number of attacks on

Workers' Headquarters district offices--the local level extensions of
Chang's organizational activities. In a telegram Keng issued to Mao,
he pointed out that while he had under him forty-eight strong and united
mass organizations, Chang could claim only just over thirty, of which
more than twenty were liaison centers from other cities.[37] Much of
Chang's support, in other words, came from contingents of organizations
that had no mass base in Shanghai.

As this strong opposition force presented itself, Chang was forced
to rely more heavily on the PLA, at first solely as a show of force.
Radio broadcasts stressed that the PLA would support the "true revolutionary leftists," and low-flying air force squadrons on January 26
dropped leaflets on the city declaring their support. On the same day
a parade of military leaders from all branches of the armed services
drove through the city in open cars as part of this demonstration of
military support.[38]

In response, the largest students' organization in the city, the Red
Revolutionaries, turned a meeting with Chang and Yao on January 27
into a struggle meeting, holding the leaders there for six hours and
trying to extort a confession that they had used troops to suppress the
mass movement.[39] In response to Chang and Yao's refusal to comply,
a group of Red Revolutionaries from Futan University raided the
Writer's Union and arrested, among others, Hsu Ching-hsien, Chang's
main propaganda writer. Chang's reaction was to send two truckloads
of PLA troops, one of police and eighteen motorcycle squads to Futan
University, where the shocked students released their prisoner and had
their headquarters occupied. This was the first time that troops had
been used in Shanghai openly to oppose the mass movement. In subsequent days the Red Revolutionaries were to retaliate, crashing a meeting
at the Liberation Daily where Chang attended, and engaging in brawls on
their campuses with the student groups supporting Chang.[40]

Stage Three--The Commune/Revolutionary Committee

The third and final stage in the assertion of Chang's organizational
authority was the establishment--despite widespread opposition--of the
Commune, which would later be renamed but survive largely unchanged
as a "Revolutionary Committee." Some writings on Shanghai during the
Cultural Revolution portray the Commune as a manifestation of "radical
utopianism";[41] but this attempt by Chang Ch'un-ch'iao to enforce some
kind of order among Shanghai's fragmented array of mass organizations

was neither distinctively "radical" nor unrealistically "utopian." Despite the utopian images conjured up by the commune in recent Chinese Marxist theorizing, the Shanghai Commune was probably supported by less than one-fourth of Shanghai's politically active working population[42] and relied heavily upon the PLA for its very survival--a survival continually threatened by the united opposition.

The Commune, in fact, marked the beginning of ever more nakedly aggressive use of force to restore order. The inauguration of the Commune was filled with references to the PLA and threats to the opposition. Chang, in his speech at the founding rally on February 5, declared that "class enemies" were using "all sorts of insidious tricks" to create difficulties for the rebels. He stressed, however, that "we also have the strong PLA standing at our side. We will break the head of anyone daring to carry out counter-revolutionary activities."[43] Liao Cheng-kuo, commander of the Shanghai PLA Garrison spoke afterwards:

> The PLA units stationed in Shanghai have made all preparations. We will ruthlessly suppress anyone who dares to undermine the Shanghai People's Commune or the proletarian Cultural Revolution.[44]

The "First Order" of the Commune stressed similar themes-- public security was to be strengthened over "irresponsible elements," and the PLA was ordered to defend "revolutionary" organizations. Wen-hui Pao's description of the inauguration included the closing line: "If anyone dares to sabotage the Shanghai People's Commune we will smash his dog's head!"[45] Similarly, another editorial on the "significance" of the Commune warned against certain "counter-revolutionaries" who are "sowing discord and dissension, confusing right and wrong, changing black and white, and reaping profit in confusion in hopes of suppressing us." For these people the editorial had a slogan: "Those who want to try the strength of the new political power of the proletariat, listen! If you want to try our strength, come forward!"[46] Simultaneous with these bellicose warnings against the United Opposition, an armed show of force was held by the local PLA garrison. A military rally pledging to defend the commune was followed by an armed parade through the city.[47]

These threats hardly intimidated the opposition groups, who formed their own organ of power--the "New Shanghai People's Commune."[48] When Keng Chin-chang noticed that the Peking press was silent about the formation of Chang's Commune--which was probably due in large measure to the strong opposition coordinated by Keng himself--he stepped up his campaign against the "suppression" by Chang and the Workers' Headquarters and held parades and rallies of his own.[49] By the middle of February his workers' forces were once again staging raids on the grass roots levels of Chang's organizational apparatus--the district branches of the Workers' Headquarters.[50]

The Commune was clearly not achieving its purpose of uniting warring groups under Chang's administration. Shanghai was once again divided into two major factions--this time over the issue of Chang's leadership--and the clashes between the two groups could do nothing but hurt production. Clearly worried about developments in Shanghai, Mao on February 12 called Chang and Yao to Peking, where he reportedly was so anxious to talk to them that he waited for them in his doorway. Mao was concerned about the charges of suppression made by delegates from Keng's First, Second, and Third Regiments.[51] He was similarly concerned about the opposition of the Red Revolutionaries and the actions of the Red Flag Army against the PLA at Lunghua Airfield.[52] He sought assurance that the student groups were still supplementing the labor supply at the docks, and in turn assured the Shanghai officials that "if that meeting is held to bombard Chang Ch'un-ch'iao we will certainly take the necessary steps and arrest people."[53] He denounced the slogan forwarded by some sectors of the Shanghai opposition--"doubt everything and overthrow everything"--as reactionary and suggested, for a variety of reasons, that the Commune form be abandoned. Most relevant to the immediate situation in Shanghai was the following consideration:

> Communes are too weak when it comes to suppressing
> counter-revolution. People have come and complained
> to me that when the Bureau of Public Security arrests
> people, they go in the front door and out the back.[54]

The major part of Mao's proposed solution to the persistent Shanghai problem was to officially change the Commune into a Revolutionary Committee of the Heilungkiang type.[55] This would have the effect of identifying Chang's leadership with the officially approved Heilungkiang model, while implicitly giving Mao's sanction to Chang's efforts to use the PLA and public security forces to restore order.

Almost simultaneous with Chang and Yao's return to Shanghai, Public Security crackdowns on the opposition had begun. The most militant of the opposition groups, the Red Flag Army--composed of demobilized soldiers and responsible for resistance to PLA takeovers

of airfields and radio stations--was officially abolished by an order of
the Public Security Bureau on February 17. [56] The Bureau raided the
headquarters of the organization and placed its leaders under arrest. [57]
A simultaneous propaganda campaign labelled Red Flag Army members
as the "scum of society" and stressed once again that "turning the spearhead of struggle" towards the PLA was intolerable and that the touchstone
for distinguishing a revolutionary from a counterrevolutionary was "attitude" towards the PLA. [58] In the wake of the actions against the Red
Flag Army, an organization of sent-down permanent Shanghai workers
who had besieged and occupied the Commune's offices were similarly
suppressed by public security forces. [59]

In the same week, the Commune announced that it would be renamed as the Shanghai Municipal Revolutionary Committee. [60] At a
restricted-admission mass rally on February 24, Chang gave a two
hour speech that was televised throughout the city and surrounding
counties. [61] Chang made two points perfectly clear: he had met with
Mao three times and had received his full support, and Mao was worried
about the tendency of the Shanghai opposition to overthrow all people in
authority. Mao, he said, felt that the line had to be drawn somewhere
and that he was drawing it at the CCRG membership--Chang himself. [62]
Further, Chang called for a halt to the attacks on the PLA and leadership cadres. Without the army, Chang asserted, nothing could be
achieved, and students and workers could not possibly run the city's
enterprises and administration by themselves. After all, Chang explained, most students had not even graduated, and he himself lacked
knowledge of finance and agriculture and was finding it difficult to man-
age the city. [63] For these reasons attacks on leading cadres in enterprises and the city administration must stop. Their activities can be
"supervised," but they must not be removed. [64]

Chang's speech, the nominal abandonment of the Commune, and
the overt suppression of opposition groups by Public Security demoral-
ized most opposition groups. Their position that Chang was a revisionist
and compromiser was undercut by Mao's now obvious support for him;
the nominal shift to a Revolutionary Committee would make further
resistance to Chang a challenge to Mao's authority; and the more
aggressive posture of public security forces made large-scale resistance increasingly hazardous. The large, unified opposition broke up
into decentralized cells of dissidents in local neighborhoods and individual workplaces. Shanghai, by the end of February, no longer had
two major factions in opposition to one another--it merely suffered from
chronic isolated "tendencies" that were the grass roots vestiges of the
former alliance against Chang.

VIII

CHANG CH'UN-CH'IAO AND THE
POLITICS OF DEMOBILIZATION

By early March the Shanghai press declared that Keng Chin-chang's organization was disintegrating and that all along it had been manipulated by the old MPC.[1] Articles explaining the significance of the Revolutionary Committee stressed the importance of the PLA, of Public Security, and of proletarian dictatorship. Student liaison offices, most notably the vociferously anti-Chang Chingkangshan, were ordered to close down and leave town.[2] With the unified opposition to his leadership eliminated as a powerful force, Chang could set himself once again to the task of restoring normal social order and production by eliminating those unforseen disruptions that had occurred during the Cultural Revolution in Shanghai--a task he had haltingly begun in the first days of January.

Now Chang Ch'un-ch'iao, with the support of the Workers' Headquarters, in effect continued the series of demobilization campaigns that he had begun in Shanghai in early January 1967. Unfailingly couched in radical sounding rhetoric and always presented as higher stages in the attacks on the bourgeois headquarters, these campaigns were actually aimed at achieving eminently practical goals--establishing labor discipline, sidetracking economic demands, returning youths and workers to the countryside, halting attacks on basic level cadres of all types, and returning students to school--all vital parts of a program to restore Shanghai's paralyzed economy and disrupted social order. By no means dogmatically attached to a utopian position, Chang did not hesitate to suppress the growing opposition to these programs from the large, militant sector of Shanghai's dissident movement--the Red Revolutionaries, the Red Flag Army, the Second Regiment of Workers, and the Workers' Third Army--the same sector that had presented the old MPC with its most outspoken opposition.

This program was characterized by its attempt to project onto a small handful of powerless former leaders those qualities that Chang wished to combat in the masses themselves. This tactic not only

65

communicated to Shanghai's population which behavior was intolerable, but it was an explicit attempt to have warring factions unite against a common, albeit symbolic, enemy. Throughout the period calls went out to "promote unity through criticism" by directing the spearhead of criticism away from cadres and mass factions and towards the "top Party persons."[3] The main obstacle of the movement was declared to be "the bourgeois reactionary line, especially the cadre policy of hitting hard at the many" (or, in other words, criticizing and removing large numbers of basic level leaders), and "only by thoroughly criticizing this line can we unite and form a great alliance to carry out the Cultural Revolution."[4] This "criticizing" took the form of a call to "settle accounts" with the former MPC handful, who allegedly had tried to sabotage the Cultural Revolution.[5]

As part of this effort, a whole series of televised struggle rallies were held in order to expose "the top Party person" and his "deputies" in the Shanghai MPC.[6] This coincided with a string of forums, rallies, and editorials proclaiming a "general offensive" of criticism against this handful.[7] A simultaneous call went out to "resume the debate that has been suppressed" by criticizing the influence of the "handful" in literary and art circles--debates reminiscent of those a year earlier under Ts'ao Ti-ch'iu's leadership.[8] By the summer of 1967 this policy of directing criticism towards a small group of former leaders had become formalized to the extent that the Central Committee in Peking specified which local leaders were to serve as symbolic targets. In the case of Shanghai, this role was filled by Ts'ao Ti-ch'iu, Ch'en P'ei-hsien, and Yang Hsi-kuang.[9]

A second characteristic of Chang's program to restore Shanghai's economy was his attempt to break down the countless small organizations that had formed earlier in Shanghai's Cultural Revolution, many of which were mere interest groups pressing specific social or economic demands. These small organizations that had proven so disruptive to Shanghai's economy were attacked for exhibiting the "guild mentality"--the tendency to form groups according to economic grievances--a mentality that "divides the working class" and "mixes people of different political viewpoints."[10] Beginning in March, a concerted effort was launched to attack the "small-group mentality" that had spawned citywide groups of bus conductors, cooks, and apprentices, and to encourage the new organizations within, and not across, individual work units, departments, and systems. Workers were to be organized into "great alliances" contained within each workplace, whose task would be to mobilize criticism against the handful of bourgeois leaders--not to agitate for redress of social and economic grievances.[11] These "great alliances" were designed to defuse spontaneous coalitions based on common interest. PLA contingents were integral parts of each local alliance, and the Workers' Headquarters--formerly a dissident mass organization but rapidly becoming an organizational arm of the Municipal Revolutionary Committee--also contributed its calming presence. These contingents, by steering debate towards officially approved issues, were to assure that individual work units were not faced, as they were in December and January, with an array of competing interest groups forwarding demands, fighting one another, and disrupting production.

In each of the areas where disruptions had become a major problem in Shanghai, Chang's administration, using the tactics outlined above, attempted gradually to restore social conditions to near normalcy.

Halting Attacks on Industrial and Administrative Cadres

In the first days after Wen-hui Pao became a dissident organ, it had called for "savage attacks upon bourgeois authorities."[12] This policy had led to the regular persecution of minor officials and authorities, who were commonly paraded through the streets in the backs of trucks, wearing placards and dunce caps. Leading cadres in Shanghai's schools, factories and offices were subjected to a merciless barrage of criticism. When unsupervised dissidents "seized power" independently in individual factories during the first days of January, either all of the management cadres were removed, or they were intimidated to such an extent that they refused to report for work.[13]

These occurrences, which were doing nothing to restore production in Shanghai, were soon to be labelled as deviations. As early as January 15, Chou En-lai and Ch'en Po-ta, referring to Shanghai at a Peking rally, urged workers not to dismiss managers but to "supervise" them.[14] In a month's time, this same practice of "overthrowing everything" was a reactionary slogan identified with the counterrevolutionary opposition to the Commune. Care must be taken, Chang's organs stressed, to distinguish between basic level cadres and "bourgeois power holders"--failure to do so is "anti-Marxist-Leninist."[15] Only a handful of these cadres were considered reactionary; the majority, Chang's organs stressed, had made only minor errors and were "basically good" and therefore should be dealt with "discriminatingly." Most of these cadres were to be welcomed as "a precious resource" of technical and leadership skills.[16] The Cultural Revolution was, after all, not a "revolution of dismissals" but an attempt at "organizational change."[17]

While Shanghai's activists were thus restrained from attacking their immediate superiors, the media urged the intimidated cadres to return to work. Editorials declared the Rebels' intention to "welcome with open arms all revolutionary cadres rising to rebel." These cadres, far from being bourgeois power holders, were actually <u>victims</u> of the "bourgeois line."[18] With this change in official line, cadres who returned would not have to fear the charge that they were "suppressing revolution by grasping production," since now it was asserted that there is no real distinction between the two.[19] Further, they no longer needed to fear the stigma of having been absent from their posts for so long, for "there is no difference between making revolution early or late."[20]

In order to become accepted back into the revolutionary fold, these cadres had to "lay bare their hearts," confess their mistakes, and join the masses in the criticism campaigns against the small handful of "bourgeois power holders."[21] In March the press began to publicize success stories of cadres who had "rebelled" and regained their former leadership posts.[22] By April, in line with the rising criticism campaign against Liu Shao-ch'i and the "handful" of his followers in the old MPC, the practice of attacking basic level cadres had been metamorphosized into a plot by bourgeois authorities: "struggling against the many in order to protect the few."[23]

Returning Students to School

As early as January 15, Chang's leadership had made a concerted effort to urge students to return to school.[24] In order to prevent the Cultural Revolution from becoming merely a "passing show," students were urged to "plunge into a new battle," return to and reopen the schools.[25] While there they were to "seize power" from counter-revolutionaries and forge the "great alliance," while applying the lenient policy towards industrial cadres to the teaching and administrative staffs of the schools.[26] This effort initially concentrated on primary and middle schools,[27] but months later Chang was urging university students to likewise stop their factional struggles, declaring his distaste for the uses to which they put Mao's "little red book":

> The reading of quotations has become nothing but a war of words. I will only read passages from the quotations which are favorable to me, but will not read anything which is unfavorable to me.[28]

Just as in the case of the attacks on cadres, undesirable behavior was traced to the influence of unnamed "bourgeois authorities." The "militant" call for students to "fight back to the school to study and make revolution" was declared to be aimed at defeating "the trick of the handful of Party people in authority and taking the capitalist road to lure students away from their schools."[29] Likewise, teachers who had been "deceived by the bourgeois line" should be allowed to join in this new "struggle"--the opening of schools.[30] Teachers and other students should not be the targets of a struggle which should be directed only towards the handful of former MPC leaders.[31]

Returning Youths to the Countryside

A simultaneous but far more intense campaign was launched to urge sent-down youths who had returned to Shanghai during the Cultural Revolution to go back to their rural villages. In early February the call went out to "fight our way back to the home villages and carry out revolution right there."[32] The criteria for distinguishing a "truly revolutionary" youth was declared to be whether or not he was willing to return to work in the countryside.[33] After a week this Shanghai campaign was given the authority of a Central directive issued on February 17.[34]

This mobilization effort included well-publicized neighborhood celebrations for those youths persuaded to return,[35] and, like the other mobilization campaigns under Chang, the youths' illegal return to Shanghai was blamed on the "handful" of former MPC leaders. Youths were urged not to fall into "the enemy's trap" by leaving their rural production posts, and those who had already been "duped" by the MPC's plot of economism were ordered to return to Sinkiang in order to smash this "current counter-plot."[36] A rash of "confessions" by youths who had returned to Shanghai invariably traced their actions to the machinations of the MPC.[37] The campaign, however, did not end with this: on February 26, only two days after its inauguration, the Municipal Revolutionary Committee had the headquarters of the organizations of returned youths closed down and confiscated their funds and property.[38]

Resolving the Issue of Worker Economic Demands

The issue of the justifiability of the temporary and contract labor system--one that had figured so decisively in the economic crisis of late December and early January--had yet to be resolved. Chiang Ch'ing had agreed on December 26 that the system of contract labor was a "corrupt" product of the bourgeois line, and the rebel-controlled Shanghai Radio had reported sympathetically as late as January 6 on efforts by temporary workers' organizations to "crush the unreasonable system."[39] As the CCRG and Chang Ch'un-ch'iao moved to restore Shanghai's economy and exercised increasing institutional control over mass organizations, however, the nonpermanent workers' demands were treated with progressively less sympathy. An unofficial Central directive declared on January 12 that the system of temporary labor was "rational in some cases," even though surely "erroneous" in others.[40] By the end of January, however, Shanghai's anti-economism "Front-line Command" declared that

> one of the biggest plots at present is to instigate workers, under the pretext of "opposing the bourgeois reactionary line", to oppose "unreasonable systems"; sabotaging the economy.[41]

Within two weeks (by February 17), the CCRG had ordered the national organizations of temporary and contract workers disbanded. Temporary workers' demands that they be given equal political rights were honored, but the economic demands did not fare as well. The CCRG had apparently decided that the system was vital to China's economy, for the system of temporary and contract labor was declared "rational" in some cases, while it was promised that the Central Committee was studying possible reforms.[42]

In little more than a week, on February 27, the Shanghai Municipal Revolutionary Committee, declaring that "bad elements" had infiltrated organizations of temporary and contract workers, closed their offices and confiscated their funds.[43] The very next day, the Revolutionary Committee reneged on the December 26 Central directive, repudiated the December 27 pact between the old MPC and the Workers' Headquarters and, urging temporary and contract workers to "destroy selfishness," announced that they were once again being laid off and that they must immediately leave their work units.[44]

A similar fate befell the demands of those permanent Shanghai workers who had returned to the city to protest the system that transferred them to rural and inland areas. Following the familiar pattern of the other campaigns to restore order and production in Shanghai, it was first asserted in mid-January that the old MPC, using the bait of "economism," had lured these sent-down workers to return to Shanghai to make "unreasonable economic requests."[45] Immediately thereafter, Chang's leadership launched a late January campaign urging workers to "fight back to the home towns to make revolution there," while criticizing those who forwarded the politically erroneous slogan "reversing the injustice of moving to the interior."[46]

Restoring Order in Shanghai's Neighborhoods

As Chang's efforts to sidetrack protest over economic issues and to curtail attacks upon industrial and administrative cadres became increasingly effective, cadres in Shanghai's neighborhoods were declared to be in a "state of upheaval."[47] Returned youths and their parents were struggling against the lane cadres responsible for mobilizing youth to the countryside and were demanding permits to remain in the city.[48] Small, local organizations of sent-down workers were adding their grievances to this wave of "unjustified economic demands" and were similarly engaged in "dragging out" the basic level cadres.[49]

As the suppression of mass organizations opposed to the Commune became more effective after February 18, opposition attacks became increasingly directed solely at these neighborhood-level leaders. Keng Chin-chang's organization, for example, had concentrated its activities in the Wusung area, where it had attacked public security stations, declared itself in power, and organized struggle meetings against lane cadres, declaring its intention to pull them down "one by one."[50] Other local organizations, like the one in the Wangchia wharf area, led violent attacks against lane cadres, reportedly raiding homes to make midnight arrests and kidnapping and beating people.[51] The activities of organizations in other neighborhoods seemed devoid of political content; many simply terrorized neighborhoods by raiding homes and stealing equipment.[52]

Chang's initial reaction to this new wave of disorder was to publish a series of strongly worded articles condemning the attacks on neighborhood cadres as the action of "bad elements itching for class revenge" directed behind-the-scenes by the "handful" of old MPC leaders. "We can criticize and educate" the neighborhood cadres, these editorials urged, "but we must not treat them as targets of struggle."[53] Instead, rebels must thoroughly repudiate the bourgeois line, "pointing the spearhead upward, not downward."[54]

These articles, instead of producing the desired effect, provoked a three-day siege and occupation of the Wen-hui Pao offices by dissident groups from the neighborhoods.[55] Thousands of these angry demonstrators accused the paper of distorting the targets of struggle and asserted that lane cadres were corrupt power-holders. They argued that all authorities had to be examined, otherwise the roots of revisionism could not be destroyed. They charged Wen-hui Pao, and by implication, Chang Ch'un-ch'iao, with trying to suppress the mass movement.[56]

Chang then took the initiative away from the attacking dissidents. Local public security stations, at times assisted by the PLA, began to arrest leaders and disband local dissident organizations.[57] At the same time, struggle rallies against the attackers of lane cadres were organized by the Public Security branches in many neighborhoods.[58] In some cases these struggle sessions were waived in favor of well-publicized public trials, in which "criminals" and "counterrevolutionaries" received terms ranging from seven to twenty years of imprisonment or hard labor for their part in orchestrating attacks on neighborhood cadres.[59] By the end of March, the situation had been quelled sufficiently for forty thousand neighborhood cadres to vow, in a televised oath-taking rally, to "bravely" return to their posts.[60]

Shanghai in the Summer of 1967

Chang's role as a stabilizing force in Shanghai's polity and economy during 1967 and his success in that role are laid into bold relief by a comparison of events in Shanghai during the summer of 1967 with those in China's other major urban centers. The period from the end of July to the first days of September were probably the most violent and bloody months of the Cultural Revolution in China--months that many observers feel led to a basic shift in Central policies toward the movement. Symbolic of the violent factionalism into which the Cultural Revolution had degenerated in most of China was the "Wuhan Incident."[61] Lasting from July 20 to August 4,[62] this series of violent events in Wuhan, which saw local military leaders defy Central orders in their efforts to intervene in mass factionalism, touched off an effort by some members of the CCRG to orchestrate attacks upon local military leaders who were reportedly "obstructing" the movement.

This effort to "drag out the handful in the army," which coincided with criticisms of Chou En-lai and attacks on the Foreign Ministry under his direction and which later was laid to efforts by CCRG members

Wang Li, Kuan Feng, Lin Chieh, and Mu Hsin, dominated Chinese politics until the beginning of September.[63] During this period, with the army partially immobilized and stripped of its unquestioned authority as a peace-keeping force, violent political clashes reached their highest peak.[64] Not until September, when the policy of encouraging mass criticism of army leaders was reversed, could the PLA begin to play an effective role in suppressing violent conflict and in providing the discipline necessary for reconstructing local institutional frameworks.[65]

In stark contrast to the events in most of China and with the opposition of many CCRG members to PLA activities, Shanghai's situation remained relatively stable and the local PLA continued to play a vital, unquestioned role in the functioning of the city's polity and economy. The local military, so central to Chang's effort to reinstate order and quell opposition to his efforts to do so, was by now firmly entrenched in the city's administrative institutions. Liao Cheng-kuo, the commander of the Shanghai Garrison, had played a central role in Chang's efforts to establish the Commune/Revolutionary Committee and had enjoyed a position as vice-chairman of the Revolutionary Committee since its establishment in February.[66] Chang Ch'un-ch'iao himself was tied into the local military hierarchy, having become in February first secretary of both the Nanking Military Region and the Shanghai district PLA Garrison.[67]

With the local PLA and Chang's administration so intimately intertwined, it is not surprising that the policy of encouraging attacks on the army made virtually no headway in Shanghai. When the first CCRG call to "drag out" representatives of the bourgeoisie in the army was issued from Peking on July 22,[68] in the midst of the "Wuhan Incident," Shanghai's media paid deference to this Central policy shift by changing the wording of its calls for attacks on the bourgeoisie to include the army as well as the Party, state, and cultural groups.[69] This shift, however, occurred in the midst of an existing local campaign to promote an upsurge of political study and formalized criticism of "capitalist roaders"-- the latest in a long series of local campaigns to eradicate surviving pockets of factional strife and opposition to Chang's leadership by promoting "unity in criticism" of China's symbolic Khrushchev.[70] In the context of Shanghai's demobilization campaigns, the CCRG-inspired effort to "drag out" PLA leaders prompted only the addition of army personnel to the symbolic list of unnamed revisionist leaders being subjected to relentless criticism in Shanghai. The calls for moves against the army, in other words, were completely adulterated, and the incendiary effects they had on other regions of China were averted in Shanghai.

Even if formal criticism of unnamed "revisionists" in the army seemed possible given this slight alteration in the wording of locally published editorials, Chang's administration made very clear that actual attacks upon PLA prestige and authority were not to be tolerated. As early as July 28, within days of the start of the CCRG moves against the army, the Shanghai media stressed the pivotal role of the PLA in supporting the "left" in Shanghai since the first days of the January Revolution.[71] The media buildup of the PLA coincided with warnings against members of disbanded organizations who, apparently inspired by events in Wuhan and elsewhere, were agitating and organizing in isolated pockets of the city to rebuild the opposition movement that Chang had suppressed. These organizations were warned that Shanghai was already under the control of "proletarian revolutionaries."[72]

To drive home these points, the Shanghai Military Control Commission held in Shanghai on August 1 a massive rally, featuring representatives of all the branches of the armed services. The PLA was saluted, once again, for supporting the left, and dissidents were explicitly warned against attacking the PLA.[73] Wang Shao-yung, a civilian vice-chairman of the Municipal Revolutionary Committee, declared at this rally the necessity to "stir up a new upsurge in supporting the Army . . . and put out still greater efforts to consolidate militant solidarity with the PLA." Wang continued,

> We proletarian revolutionaries of Shanghai still remember clearly that in the great stormy revolution of January, the PLA units stationed in Shanghai, acting on Chairman Mao's instructions, directly intervened in the local great proletarian cultural revolution, thereby ensuring the smooth development of the great proletarian cultural revolution. Since the seizure and mastery of power by the proletariat, the PLA has rendered tremendous support to the proletariat in the struggle for consolidating and strengthening the dictatorship of the proletariat.[74]

The message that "the PLA is a powerful mainstay for proletarian dictatorship" was painfully obvious, as was the idea that "without a people's Army, there is nothing for the people."[75] Thus, on August 1, in the midst of CCRG-inspired attacks upon the PLA and a full month before this Central policy was reversed, Wang Shao-yung called for a movement to "Support the Army and Cherish the People" so that Shanghai could become "an iron bastion of Army-people unity."[76]

When minor, isolated attacks upon army personnel and other Revolutionary Committee authority figures did occur, the Shanghai media seized upon these events and built them up into highly publicized affairs. At the Shanghai Diesel Engine Plant, apparently one of those isolated pockets that still suffered from chronic factional infighting, a comparatively minor incident occurred on August 3 that was to touch off an official furor greatly disproportionate to its actual seriousness.

A dissident group at the plant known as "Lien Szu" had resisted attempts by representatives of the PLA and Workers' Headquarters to "seize power" and redirect political activities among the factory workers. The problem at this plant had been serious and persistent enough for the Municipal Revolutionary Committee to give it specialized attention. On August 2 the Committee released an open letter to the workers in the plant in hopes of overcoming the stubborn political resistance of this local organization. When representatives of the Revolutionary Committee, accompanied by a PLA escort and a contingent of journalists from Shanghai's newspapers, radio and television networks, arrived on August 3 in several propaganda trucks bearing bundles of this open letter, they received less than a warm welcome. A civilian representative of the Revolutionary Committee, met at the plant gate by members of "Lien Szu," was given a sound thrashing, and PLA troops who tried to intervene were also surrounded and attacked by kicking and swinging workers. As the scuffle escalated, the busy journalists had their cameras smashed, and the propaganda trucks were overturned and looted.[77]

Compared to the widespread violence in Wuhan, Canton, and elsewhere during this same period, this was indeed a minor outbreak, but the Municipal Revolutionary Committee reacted swiftly and forcefully to the "Diesel Plant Incident," making it the cause for an August campaign to eliminate these isolated pockets of resistance. The day after the incident, the city administration held a mass protest rally and parade, the Workers' Headquarters issued a public denunciation, and Wen-hui Pao and Chieh-fang Jih-pao ran separate belligerent editorials attacking the leaders of "Lien Szu."[78] Chief among the charges made against this group was that they had dared to oppose "representatives of the armed forces at the plant" and that they had "physically assaulted the PLA commanders and fighters."[79] Over the next few days the incident remained the focus of media efforts, with repeated descriptions of the exemplary conduct of the PLA and specific warnings to the "Lien Szu" dissidents gradually fading into a more general media effort to praise PLA peacekeeping efforts and to underscore that

we do not allow any person to use pretexts to sow discord
between the Army and the people with the aim of pointing
the spearhead at the great PLA, undermining the proletarian dictatorship, and disrupting the order of the revolution. [80]

Except for a brief notice on August 13 that the situation at the Diesel
Plant was under the control of PLA propaganda teams, [81] the "Lien Szu"
incident, having served its pedagogical function, was quickly dropped
as media lashings of "China's Khrushchev" and calls to strengthen public security resumed. [82]

With strong organizational ties linking him to the local military,
and with the military continuing to provide him with essential support
at crucial points in Shanghai's Cultural Revolution, Chang Ch'un-ch'iao
did not join in the summer attacks against the army inspired by his
CCRG colleagues. Any attacks against the PLA in Shanghai would simultaneously undermine the foundation of Chang's political authority. This
organizational link illuminates the reasons for the split that occurred
in the so-called "radical" faction of the top national leadership in late
August. Wang Li and his colleagues in Peking, free of such organizational links to the PLA in their positions on the CCRG, forwarded
attacks on the army which directly threatened Chang's power in Shanghai and the success of his local efforts. The Shanghai leadership subsequently sided with the national military leadership in its dispute with
the young anti-army "radicals," with Yao Wen-yuan himself penning in
early September what is considered by one observer to be the "coup de
grace" against the Wang Li group--an article denouncing a conspiracy
of "ultra-leftists" in the Central leadership. [83]

Chang Ch'un-ch'iao, in sum, effectively isolated Shanghai from
the CCRG-inspired efforts to attack the provincial army leadership and
successfully averted the occurrence of widespread violence that plagued
most of China at the time. At a crucial point in Cultural Revolution
politics, Chang sided with the military leadership in its national policy
dispute with the "radicals" in Peking, providing crucial support necessary for defeating his once-close political associates.

IX

CONCLUSIONS

Our account of the complex array of political and social conflicts that comprised Shanghai's January Revolution, and of the efforts of one individual--Chang Ch'un-ch'iao--to foster, direct and shape these conflicts, differs from previous interpretations in several important respects. These interpretive differences are directly related to a set of theoretical perspectives that seem particularly applicable to the January Revolution, and perhaps to Chinese politics and society in general. The actions of elite political actors in Shanghai are illuminated by an understanding of the organizational networks in which they operate, just as the political mobilization of the population cannot be adequately understood apart from the underlying social divisions and conflicts that determine the form this mobilization will take. The actions of an individual political actor like Chang Ch'un-ch'iao are thus constrained both by organizational positions and responsibilities, and by often unpredictable mass responses to political mobilization. This perspective generates some new insights into the strategies and political aims of "radical" politicians in China both during and after the Cultural Revolution and underscores some very real obstacles that faced efforts to induce social change in China through these political methods.

Interpretive Shifts

Past interpretations of the Cultural Revolution have contended that provincial political leaders used a variety of methods to preserve their own political power and dull the effects of the movement in their areas.[1] Relatedly, Shanghai's January Revolution is often interpreted as an attempt to break through this local resistance to the developing mass movement through an outright "power seizure" by mass political organizations.[2] The actions of local municipal elites, in other words, are viewed as acts of obstruction, while the January Revolution is seen as an attempt to overcome the obstacles to the movement presented by the defensive actions of local leaders. The subsequent attempt to

77

establish a Commune is consequently viewed as an episode of romantic utopianism that would later be tempered by a dose of political reality and a retreat from the Commune and radicalism.[3]

The January Revolution. Closer examination of existing evidence for the events in Shanghai has demanded a number of revisions in this dominant view. First, the actions of such local municipal officials as Ts'ao Ti-ch'iu suggest that, far from actively obstructing the movement, local leaders may actually have promoted it in good faith in its earlier stages. Subsequent opposition within the Shanghai MPC to workers' organizations was not only supported by CCRG policy at the time doubts were voiced but was also based upon accurate predictions of the disruptive effects such organizations would have upon Shanghai's economy. The old Shanghai MPC, in fact, was very careful to follow existing Central guidelines on the Cultural Revolution and followed, albeit with some protestation, each progressive policy shift until it could no longer exercise effective leadership over the burgeoning dissident movements. Far from systematically and successfully obstructing the Cultural Revolution in Shanghai, the MPC progressively lost control over events in the city--a process contributing to the total political and economic collapse of December 1966.

Secondly, the source of this collapse was not, as has so often been suggested, manipulation and sabotage on the part of the MPC leadership and its followers.[4] Shanghai's collapse, on the contrary, was due on the one hand to progressively daring CCRG policies that unleashed unforeseen economic demands and surprisingly violent and persistent factional infighting and on the other hand to Central prohibitions against obstructing the movement which prevented the MPC from acting as a stabilizing force. The array of demands forwarded by various workers' organizations, further, required no encouragement by municipal leaders. The outbreak of "economism" had observable roots in shifts in China's employment structure, just as the subsequent mass factionalism had its foundations in the stratified system of distribution of wages and benefits.[5]

The January Revolution, thirdly, was by no means a radical attempt to break through local obstructions placed on the movement but was from the beginning an effort coordinated by Chang Ch'un-ch'iao to control and redirect an unexpectedly violent and benefit-oriented mass movement that had halted Shanghai's economy and threatened to discredit Cultural Revolution policies. The retreat from the disruptive CCRG policies forwarded during the fall of 1966 thus began with Chang's active, full-time reinvolvement in Shanghai politics during the first days of January. The subsequent Commune was consequently not a manifestation of radical utopianism[6] but was part, albeit an unsuccessful and short-lived one, of a continuing effort to restore order and production in China's most important industrial and commercial city. As part of this effort, Chang's propaganda apparatus generated the interpretation of MPC actions and of the January Revolution that has colored in varying degrees subsequent Western accounts.

Chang Ch'un-ch'iao and Chinese "Radicalism". Chang's actions during Shanghai's Cultural Revolution, finally, do not fit with a common unidimensional conception of him as a "radical ideologue" or a political "romantic." Chang's task in Shanghai was not to engineer a utopian Commune but to forge some sort of political unity by any means in order to remedy the economic and administrative paralysis that had befallen the city. Reinstating labor discipline, redirecting factional energies, sidetracking social grievances and economic demands, and suppressing incorrigible opposition--Chang's actions belied an eminently practical politician, vitally concerned with restricting the unexpectedly violent and destructive dimensions of a mass movement that he himself had helped to initiate. Apparently aware that making revolution was indeed not the same as drafting an essay, Chang utilized a flexible political strategy mandated by actual conditions in Shanghai.

Chang's hard-line tactics were not a repudiation of his long held political beliefs, nor were they necessarily inconsistent with a "Maoist" position. Any leader or group of leaders who advocate giving workers and other citizens the right to criticize their superiors and participate in basic level decisions bears the responsibility for assuring that the ferment and disruption of routine that results from the exercise of these rights will remain both constructive and limited. Any analysis of Chinese politics either during or after the Cultural Revolution that assumes radicals are solely for "mobilization and disruption" while moderates are for "order and production"[7] will, for these reasons, mislead rather than enlighten. Chang Ch'un-ch'iao--undoubtedly a Chinese "radical"-- has shown both the willingness and ability to take firm measures to moderate the course of a mass movement in order to assure that the movement does not lose its desired direction.

Theoretical Perspectives

While demanding revisions in some previous interpretations of Chinese politics during the Cultural Revolution, this case study--of elite political behavior in an organization undergoing extreme uncertainty and set within a social system experiencing massive unrest--suggests some theoretical perspectives that might potentially contribute to our understanding of the contemporary Chinese political and social system. Organizational and social structure, specifically, need to be recognized as important determinants of the form conflict takes in a political system--even at the elite level.

Organizational Structure and Political Conflict. Individual political actors engage in politics within a complex organizational network, especially in the minutely organized Chinese political system. The organizational setting of individual political actions has repeatedly emerged as an explanatory factor in our analysis of the January Revolution.

Organizational positions and responsibilities, firstly, can provide relative freedom to advocate certain political positions or they can severely circumscribe options. Lodged first within a local propaganda bureaucracy and then within the CCRG--neither position involving direct involvement in the functioning of the economy--Chang initially was afforded the freedom to advocate the formation of workers' organizations and attacks upon "revisionists," while having to wrestle with little more than the political ideals involved. Ts'ao Ti-ch'iu and other MPC officials, on the other hand, constantly confronted with the near-impossible task of reconciling Chang-inspired policies with the normal functioning of the economy also demanded by Central authorities, were acutely aware of the contradictions and potential dangers of these policies and expressed these difficulties in complaints to Central authorities. When Chang inherited Ts'ao Ti-ch'iu's organizational responsibilities in January 1967, he very quickly exhibited almost identical concerns about the maintenance of production and order and, unlike Ts'ao, actually moved to suppress dissident political activity. In an ironic reversal of roles, when Wang Li and his CCRG associates, enjoying the same sort of organizational freedom earlier enjoyed by Chang, urged attacks upon local "revisionist" army officials, Chang, acting as a responsible local official carefully guarding production and civil order, averted such attacks in Shanghai and took political moves against his CCRG associates.

Disrupted organizational routine, secondly, was an important contributing factor to the behavior of Shanghai's municipal elite as the

Cultural Revolution unfolded. In the uncertain political atmosphere created by the earlier purge of P'eng Chen and other Peking Party officials, local Party officials in Shanghai were careful not to be found acting in noncompliance with Central policy. In adhering closely to existing Party policy at each stage of the movement, however, the MPC doomed itself not only to losing control over the local situation but also to being vulnerable to appearing as opponents of CCRG policy. While existing official policy usually left local administrators uncertain of proper ways to deal with the burgeoning dissident movement, Central policy also shifted rapidly, undermining their exercise of local leadership and authority. Thus, in refusing to recognize the Workers' Headquarters and in opposing in principle organizations of workers in early November, for example, the MPC was acting on clearly established CCRG guidelines. Within days after the MPC took an official stand on this issue, however, official policy towards workers' organizations changed, undermining MPC authority and creating the illusion that it had obstructed the movement by contravening Central guidelines.

Finally, the turbulent social environment of the local Party organization constantly confronted the local Party with novel problems for which Central directives left it unprepared. The emerging dissident movements often forwarded issues for which the CCRG would not provide an official policy until weeks later. The local Party organization, torn between its need to act decisively and its fear of acting in contravention of Central directives, placed progressively greater emphasis on the latter concern, gradually abdicating decision-making responsibilities and further arousing dissident opposition. In other words, in a period where Centrally-articulated goals were less than clear, but where there were strict sanctions against "obstructing" the movement, and where the burgeoning array of social movements created a shifting and novel array of issues and problems, the local Party organization chose as a course of preservation not to make important decisions--a course which hastened both the impending chaos and its own political doom.

Social Structure and Political Conflict. While political behavior of elites is shaped and constrained by the organizational networks within which it occurs, it is also indirectly influenced by existing social structure. When calls for political mobilization in Shanghai fell upon a laboring population experiencing basic shifts and strains in its occupational structure, the resulting social cleavages and mass political conflicts decisively altered the thrust of the elite-inspired movement--an event that demanded elite response. Dissident groups within Shanghai's population took calls for criticism of revisionist leadership as cause for expression of basic discontents with the evolving social and economic system in which they lived and worked. Chang Ch'un-ch'iao, as a result, had to shift his activities from that of urging attacks upon authorities to that of quelling disorder and squelching economic demands--in other words, to suppress and redirect a mass movement that had adopted aims quite different from those he had envisaged for it. Independent mass political activity, in short, decisively altered the course envisaged by political elites for the Cultural Revolution, significantly shifted the range of issues under conflict, and required a series of defensive political maneuvers to head off and redirect the surprisingly virulent social movement.

The occurrence of "economism" in Shanghai underscores the important impact of a continually evolving social structure upon political conflict in the world's largest experiment in politically induced social change. The lines of division of contending groups in Shanghai, further, suggest that China's socialist form of industrial growth may be spawning historically unique social divisions for which both existing Chinese Marxist analyses and standard Western theories--both heavily influenced by observations of capitalist industrialization--may be inadequate. The exploration of the links between this form of industrialization, its related class divisions and social tensions, and the subsequent limitations these new divisions place upon elite-inspired attempts at inducing social change, remains a relatively unexplored but vitally important area of research.

Chang Ch'un-ch'iao and the Politics of Social Change

Chang's involvement in Shanghai's January Revolution, finally, points to some basic contradictions in the political strategy he and his colleagues have used to induce continued change in China's political and social system. This strategy requires its practitioners to act as instigators and managers of social and political conflict. While stimulating political conflict in Shanghai, Chang inadvertently raised the hopes and expectations of the relatively disadvantaged sectors of society, only to disappoint these hopes in the short run by subsequently declaring them to be illegitimate and their pursuit counterrevolutionary. In doing so, he earned the opposition of a major portion of the dissident movement and was able to maintain his political authority only through the decisive intervention of Mao and the PLA. While having thus alienated a significant portion of his original mass constituency, Chang was still heir to a legacy of resentment by permanent, unionized workers whose interests were threatened by the policies he had forwarded, not to mention the animosity of administrative officials at all levels--especially that of such former provincial officials as Ts'ao Ti-ch'iu--some of whom were apparently harrassed and sacked with rather flimsy political justification.

As a proponent of continuing social change through these political methods, Chang thus had to play a difficult balancing game between mobilization and demobilization, disruption and order. In attempting to use this strategy in the following decade, Chang was faced with the continuing problems of assuring that mobilized groups did not move in unexpected directions and of maintaining production during such periods of mobilization. He continued, further, to be confronted with the dangers of alienating mobilized groups whose demands go unmet, and with the prospect of accumulating animosities of privileged sectors of Chinese society and of the officials at all levels whose interests suffer in the course of these mobilization campaigns. It is an extremely difficult strategy to use effectively over a prolonged period and is a strategy that was probably repudiated--along with Chang Ch'un-ch'iao--only thirty days after the death of Mao Tse-tung.

CHRONOLOGY OF EVENTS

June 8, 1966   Media attacks on local cultural figures begin. Ho Lu-ting and Ch'en Ch'i-t'ung are first targets.

June 10   Ts'ao Ti-ch'iu delivers militant speech at mass rally inaugurating Shanghai's Cultural Revolution. Chang Ch'un-ch'iao present at rostrum.

June 11   Historian Chou Ku-ch'eng denounced and linked to the purged Peking cultural official Chou Yang.

June 14   Chou Hsin-fang, playwright colleague of Wu Han, denounced in Shanghai.

June 25   Li Chun-min, leader of local literary circles and director of Chunghua Publishing Company, denounced and linked with Chou Yang.

June 30   Chang attends mass rally in Shanghai commemorating founding of CCP.

July 1-31   Criticisms of cultural figures continue.

July 26   Chiang Ch'ing, in a speech at Peking University, mentions Chang Ch'un-ch'iao as vice-chairman of new Central Cultural Revolution Group.

August 2-12   Eleventh Plenum in Peking.

August 11   Chang Ch'un-ch'iao, Yao Wen-yuan, and Nich Yuan-tzu present at rostrum of huge rally at Tienanmen Square in Peking.

85

August 12	Mao delivers closing speech of Eleventh Plenum urging local leaders to correct their errors and encourage the student movement.
August 13	Nieh Yuan-tzu calls Ch'ang Hsi-p'ing, Secretary of Education in the Shanghai MPC, a revisionist.
August 16	Ts'ao Ti-ch'iu returns to Shanghai from Eleventh Plenum. Chang Ch'un-ch'iao remains in Peking. Ts'ao defends Ch'ang Hsi-p'ing.
August 18	Chang Ch'un-ch'iao at rostrum at Tienanmen rally.
August 19	Ts'ao Ti-ch'iu speaks at huge Shanghai rally inaugurating active Red Guard movement. Calls for attacks on bourgeois authorities.
August 22	Red Guard activities begin. People wearing Western clothes harrassed; buildings on the Bund defaced; streets renamed; churches, homes of former capitalists raided.
August 24	Ts'ao, in a speech at Futan University, urges students to be sure to have solid evidence before denouncing someone.
August 25	Dissident students from Futan stage midnight raid on Shanghai Drama Academy. Repulsed by a group of Tibetan students.
August 26	Student majority at Futan denounces dissidents, and invites Ts'ao to speak at Futan that evening. Ts'ao declares that the dissident group confused two types of contradictions.
August 26	Peking Red Guards begin to arrive in Shanghai. Warmly welcomed by MPC reception.
August 27	Chang speaks to Peking Red Guards in Peking.
August 27	Peking Red Guards in Shanghai make demands upon MPC for printing and communications equipment. Demands refused.

August 28   Peking Red Guards demonstrate in front of MPC
                   offices.

August 28-29   Shanghai media praises discipline of Tibetan students
                   from Drama Academy, stresses that reasoning,
                   not force, should characterize struggle.

August 30   Peking Red Guards hold rally at Culture Square,
                   Shanghai. Declare war on Ts'ao.

August 31   Chang alongside Mao on rostrum at huge Tienanmen
                   Red Guard rally.

September 2-3   Peking students stage sit-in at MPC offices. Media
                   stresses struggle through reason.

September 4   Peking students storm MPC offices.

September 4   Ts'ao delivers evening speech denouncing violence
                   but urges Shanghai population not to retaliate
                   against Peking students. Dissident students de-
                   clare Ts'ao's speech a "reign of white terror."

September 5   Radio broadcasts Ts'ao's speech welcoming Red
                   Guards from other localities, urging students not
                   to be overemotional.

September 7   People's Daily warns students not to interfere with
                   production.

September 15   Chang Ch'un-ch'iao attends mass rally in Peking.
                   Chou En-lai and Lin Piao stress that factories and
                   fields are off limits to Red Guards.

September 24   After a series of MPC meetings, Ts'ao Ti-ch'iu sends
                   a telegram of complaint to Peking, claiming that
                   Peking students were disrupting production.

September 30   Ts'ao gives a speech at evening reception commomo-
                   rating founding of People's Republic and urges
                   reconciliation of revolution and production. Chang
                   attends similar reception in Peking.

October 1   Peking Red Guards ordered to return to capital. Ts'ao speaks to approving crowds at National Day rally. Chang attends similar rally in Peking.

October 6   Chang makes a speech to rally of Red Guards and urges spread of Cultural Revolution to Shanghai's military academies.

October 7   Chang addresses meeting of Fukien Red Guards in Peking and is accompanied by Kuan Feng. Chang urges students not to be intimidated by suppression.

October 8-25   Central Party Work Conference. Criticisms of local responses to Red Guard movement. Self-criticisms of Liu Shao-ch'i and Teng Hsiao-p'ing.

October 25   Mao delivers closing speech of meeting, admits that havoc created by students was unforeseen, and urges local leaders to improve their relations with the students.

November 3   Chang attends mammoth Tienanmen rally and appears on rostrum with Mao, Lin Piao, Chou En-lai, Ch'en Po-ta, Liu Shao-ch'i, and Teng Hsiao-p'ing.

November 8   Representatives of newly formed Workers' General Headquarters (WGHQ) send delegates to MPC offices and demand recognition and material aid. Demands refused.

November 9   WGHQ inauguration rally in Shanghai's Culture Square.

November 10   Shanghai media reminds population that revolutionary activities must take place outside working hours.

November 10   MPC rejects five additional WGHQ demands. Workers occupy Peking-bound passenger train and declare intention to see Mao. Train halted outside the city. Telegram from Ch'en Po-ta persuades over half the workers to return to their jobs. Chang Ch'un-ch'iao reported at Peking rally.

November 11   Workers remain on train. Chang attends mass rally
in Peking and speaks to meeting of Red Guards,
declaring that students must approach factories
with care.

November 12   Chang dispatched to Shanghai to negotiate return of
workers. Signs their demands and grants recog-
nition in return for a pledge not to leave production posts.

November 13   Chang attends inauguration rally of WGHQ. Over
four hundred workers, led by Keng Chin-chang,
leave for Peking to protest Ch'en Po-ta's telegram.

November 14   Chang and Ts'ao leave together for Soochow, where
they meet Keng's regiment and make further con-
cessions in exchange for workers' return.

November 17-24 Series of MPC meetings attended by Chang. Chang
criticized for handling of workers. MPC officials
warn that workers' organizations will damage productivity and encourage large-scale disorder.

November 20   Nieh Yuan-tzu arrives in Shanghai.

November 22   Nieh Yuan-tzu tells Culture Square rally that MPC
Education Secretary Ch'ang Hsi-p'ing is a revision-
ist and that he is being protected by Ts'ao and
Teng Hsiao-p'ing.

November 25   Nieh declares intention at mass rally to bring down
the MPC and urges unity of all dissidents in
Shanghai for that purpose.

November 25   Chang Ch'un-ch'iao leaves for Peking.

November 26   Red Revolutionaries demand that 650 thousand copies
of Nieh's speech be printed and distributed by
Liberation Daily.

November 28   Chang attends CCP rally in Peking. Central-provin-
cial conference on industrial production begins.
Ma T'ien-shui represents the Shanghai MPC.

November 29	Group of Red Revolutionaries stage late night raid on post office in Shanghai and demand that it distribute their tabloid.
November 30	Rebuffed by post office, Red Revolutionaries march to Liberation Daily offices and occupy building.
December 1-4	Red Revolutionaries occupy building. Hostile crowds collect outside. Several attempts to storm building. Moderate workers distribute leaflets denouncing dissident actions.
December 5	MPC signs demands of Red Revolutionaries.
December 6	Scarlet Guards founded at mass rally, denounces dissident movement and capitulation of MPC. WGHQ claims Scarlets controlled by MPC.
December 8	MPC orders Red Revolutionaries' tabloid distributed. Fighting between Scarlets and WGHQ begins in individual factories.
December 9	Central directive urges maintenance of production and adherence to eight-hour day.
December 10	Postal workers stage walk-out to avoid distributing dissident tabloid.
December 10	WGHQ declares postal-worker strike incited by MPC, demands and receives Ts'ao's signature on additional demands. Red Revolutionaries hold struggle meeting against acting Propaganda Secretary Yang Hsi-kuang in Workers' Stadium. MPC approves purge of Yang.
December 13	Chang Ch'un-ch'iao meets with Red Guards in Peking.
December 18-19	Chang attends Red Guard rallies.
December 21	WGHQ declares intention to obtain removal of Ts'ao Ti-ch'iu and Ch'en P'ei-hsien.
December 23	Chang receives delegation from WGHQ in Peking.

December 23	Scarlets hold mass rally, denounce MPC for signing WGHQ demands, and obtain Ts'ao's signature on a list of their own demands.
December 25	Ts'ao formally repudiates his signature on Scarlet demands at mass WGHQ rally.
December 26	Sent-down permanent workers and suburban peasants begin to flow into city from surrounding counties to forward economic demands. Stage sit-in at major intersection.
December 26	Chiang Ch'ing meets with delegation of contract and temporary laborers in Peking and denounces the labor system as inspired by Liu Shao-ch'i. CCRG issues directive, published in JMJP, demanding that laid-off temporary laborers be reinstated and authorizing payment of back wages.
December 26	Both Scarlets and Rebels make unsuccessful attempts to close down each other's headquarters.
December 27	Organizations of sent-down students present demands to MPC and stage sit-in at major intersection.
December 27	WGHQ obtains MPC signature on an agreement to reinstate temporary and contract laborers and to pay back wages.
December 28	Chang attends massive Red Guard rally at Peking Workers' Stadium.
December 28	Scarlets demonstrate at MPC offices, declaring intention to settle accounts with Ts'ao Ti-ch'iu. Demonstration attacked by WGHQ contingent. Deaths reported.
December 30-31	Scarlets set out en masse to protest WGHQ behavior in Peking. Declare general strike. Intercepted at Kunshan by WGHQ contingent. Violence again ensues.
December 31	Rail traffic paralyzed by absence of workers, breaks in rail lines, and sabotage of signal system.

January 1, 1967   Delegation of rebels from <u>Wen-hui Pao</u> obtains permission to seize power in their paper.

January 3   <u>WHP</u> taken over by dissidents on staff.

January 4   Chang flies to Shanghai and meets with <u>WHP</u> staff.
Returns to Peking later the same day.

January 5   Runs on Shanghai banks begin. <u>WHP</u>'s "Message to
the Shanghai People" claims that MPC officials
incited economism among workers and are responsible for industrial breakdown. Urges workers to
return to job. Nonpermanent workers hold rally.

January 6   Chang Ch'un-ch'iao returns permanently to Shanghai.
Televised mass rally humiliates top MPC officials,
strips them of their posts.

January 6   Armed guards posted at banks and other important
buildings.

January 6   <u>WHP</u> reports sympathetically on January 5 mass rally
of temporary and contract laborers, declares goal
of tearing down the labor system.

January 7   Workers and students sent to rural areas protest at
MPC offices.

January 8   <u>WHP</u> editorial urges workers to maintain production.

January 9   <u>WHP</u>'s "Urgent Message" urges workers to return to
posts, forbids economic demands, occupations of
buildings, and urges Public Security forces to keep
order.

January 11   Central Committee issues greetings to Shanghai rebels
and congratulates them for upholding production and
maintaining order.

January 12   Chang Ch'un-ch'iao addresses mass rally of dissident
forces, reads congratulatory telegrams from Cen-
tral authorities.

January 15	Keng Chin-chang's dissident groups seize control of sections of city.
January 17	Media carries anti-economism editorials for tenth straight day.
January 18	Media urges workers to return bonuses and back wages and directs sent-down students and workers to return to the countryside.
January 20	Editorials attempt to blame old MPC for abuses in system of mobilizing youth for rural labor.
January 21	Accounts of Scarlet detachments returning in defeat from Peking.
January 23	Situation at harbor declared "near-normal."
January 24	Chang prepares meeting of all dissident groups to make plans for Commune. Rebuffed by groups led by Keng Chin-chang. Keng crashes preparatory meeting and argues loudly at rostrum with Wang Hung-wen. Meeting has to be adjourned.
January 25	Mass rally of temporary and contract laborers airs grievances and declares intention to "tear down the unreasonable system."
January 26	Shanghai Air Force squadrons drop leaflets in support of Chang over the city. First group of youths to return to Sinkiang given well-publicized sendoff.
January 29	Red Revolutionaries hold Chang and Yao for four hours, trying to extort an admission that they were suppressing the mass movement. Later kidnap Chang's speechwriter but are arrested by PLA units sent to Futan University.
January 30	Keng Chin-chang's forces attack Chang's neighborhood level organizations and district level WGHQ offices.
February 1	Chiang Ch'ing and Ch'i Pen-yu meet with dissidents in Peking and urge them to "smash" the title of chiefs, saying there will be no need for chiefs in the future.

February 2   Telegram from Peking arrives to advise Red Revolutionaries that Chang Ch'un-ch'iao is considered a "true revolutionary leftist" by the CCRG.

February 3   Keng Chin-chang launches propaganda campaign in order to prevent establishment of Chang's Commune, forms united organ of all anti-Chang dissident forces.

February 5   Commune declared at mass rally, army pledges support, warns opposition.

February 5-7 Localized clashes between demonstrators for and against Commune. Opposition forces begin to attack street level cadres.

February 7   Parents of mobilized youths organize and begin to criticize street level neighborhood cadres.

February 7   "First Order" of Commune calls for "ruthless suppression" of counterrevolutionaries. Counterrevolutionaries are defined as all those in opposition to the Commune. Call for strengthening of public security, and for end to attacks on neighborhood cadres.

February 9   Military rally demonstrating support for the Commune. Troops parade through city in show of armed force.

February 9   Keng Chin-chang sends delegates to Peking to protest Chang's actions and expose Chang's lack of mass support.

February 12   Chang and Yao summoned to Peking by Mao to discuss the local situation. Mao advises a change to a Revolutionary Committee and a strengthening of public security.

February 15   While Chang and Yao away, opposition forces launch raids on district branches of the WGHQ.

February 17   Public Security forces raid and close the headquarters of two large opposition organizations, media denounces their leadership.

February 17	Central directive abolishes national organization of temporary and contract laborers.
February 18	Chang returns to Shanghai. Shanghai's district level leadership begins door-to-door search for returned students.
February 19	Cadres urged to return to posts, told they have nothing to fear.
February 21	Leaders of local movements to attack neighborhood cadres arrested and sentenced in highly publicized mass trials.
February 22	Large opposition rally and parade.
February 22	Warnings from official media that the PLA is ready to suppress all opposition.
February 23	Rally announced to inaugurate Revolutionary Committee, later postponed.
February 24	Mass rally announcing establishment of Commune. Televised speeches by Chang and PLA officials.
February 24	Public Security arrests more leaders of opposition groups.
February 27	Anti-Chang Chingkangshan Red Guard liaison organization ordered to close and leave town.
February 27	Offices of organization of temporary and contract laborers closed down and funds and property confiscated.
February 28	Public Security arrests of opposition leaders in Nanshih and Wusung districts.
March 1	PLA contingents begin to move into all organizations to assert order.
March 1	Revolutionary Committee repudiates December 27 agreement between the WGHQ and the old MPC and

orders originally laid off workers to leave their places of employment.

March 2   Teachers and students ordered to return to school.

March 7   Returned youths ordered to go back to their country-side production posts.

March 10   Final thirteen Red Guard liaison groups bid farewell to Shanghai.

March 18   Series of televised struggle rallies against former MPC officials begins.

March 20   Establishment of first district level Revolutionary Committee announced.

March 29   Televised oath-taking rally, neighborhood level cadres pledge to "bravely return to their posts."

April 3   Intensive campaign to criticize the "top Party person" taking the capitalist road in China begins. Liu Shao-ch'i's "On the Cultivation of a Communist" criticized.

NOTES

Chapter I

1. See, for example, the following accounts, all of which share the assumption that the existing municipal leadership tried consistently to suppress the movement:

Neale Hunter, Shanghai Journal: An Eyewitness Account of the Cultural Revolution (Boston: Beacon, 1969), esp. pp. 294-98.

Vivienne B. Shue, "Shanghai After the January Storm," in The Cultural Revolution in the Provinces (Cambridge: Harvard East Asian Monographs, 1971).

Gerald Tannenbaum, "The 1967 January Revolution Recounted," Eastern Horizon, 7, no. 3 (May-June 1968): 7-25.

Victor Nee, "Revolution and Bureaucracy: Shanghai in the Cultural Revolution," in China's Uninterrupted Revolution, ed. Victor Nee and James Peck (New York: Pantheon, 1975), pp. 322-414.

Jean Daubier, A History of the Chinese Cultural Revolution (New York: Vintage, 1974), pp. 115-34.

Jack Chen, Inside the Cultural Revolution (New York: Macmillan, 1975), pp. 244-57.

Exceptions to this rule are:

K. S. Karol, The Second Chinese Revolution (New York: Hill and Wang, 1974), pp. 206-18.

Evelyn Anderson, "Shanghai: The Masses Unleashed," Problems of Communism, 47, no. 1 (January-February 1968): 12-28.

Other writings, although not sharing the same assumptions, have not challenged the dominant interpretation directly:

Chapter I Notes

Lynn T. White III, "Shanghai's Polity During the Cultural Revolution," in The City in Communist China, ed. John Lewis (Stanford: Stanford University Press, 1971): 325-70.

Lynn T. White III, "Leadership in Shanghai, 1955-69," in Elites in the People's Republic of China, ed. Robert Scalapino (Seattle: University of Washington Press, 1972): 302-77 (hereafter cited as Elites).

For example, in this second article (Elites, p. 349) White refers the reader to the writings of Hunter, Anderson, and Tannenbaum for a general overview and interpretation of the Cultural Revolution in Shanghai.

2. See, for example, the accounts by Tannenbaum (p. 16), the introduction by Ezra Vogel to The Cultural Revolution in the Provinces (p. 2), and Nee (pp. 328-30).

3. See, for example, Tannenbaum (p. 15), Nee (pp. 331-37), and Daubier (pp. 124-27).

4. See "'Down with Everything'--'Gang of Four's' Scheme to Sabotage the Great Proletarian Cultural Revolution," Peking Review, 25 March 1977: 13-16; and "Instigating Armed Conflicts--'Gang of Four's' Scheme to Sabotage the Great Cultural Revolution," Peking Review, 8 April 1977: 20-22.

Chapter II Notes

1. Chang Ch'un-ch'iao, "On Exercising All-Round Dictatorship Over the Bourgeoisie," Peking Review, 4 April 1975: 5-11.

2. Union Research Service Biographical Service 883, 2 June 1964; and Who's Who in Communist China (Hong Kong: Union Research Institute, 1969), pp. 20-21.

3. Chieh-fang Jih-Pao, 9 December 1951; Shanghai Ta Kung Pao, 22 August 1952, in SCMP 409: 20-23.

4. Lynn T. White III, "Leadership in Shanghai, 1955-69," in Elites, ed. Scalapino, pp. 302-77, 338. For an account of the Hu Feng

Chapter II Notes

campaign, see Merle Goldman, Literary Dissent in Communist China (New York: Atheneum, 1971).

5. By late 1953 Chang was managing director of Chieh-fang Jih-pao (CFJP, 19 October 1953), and in the ensuing two years he sat on increasingly important local committees. By 1955 he was acting secretary of the Literary and Art Work Committee of the Propaganda Department of the Shanghai Municipal Party Committee and was vice-chairman of the Shanghai branch of the All-China Federation of Journalists. URS Bio 883, and Who's Who, pp. 20-21.

6. See Roderick MacFarquhar, Origins of the Cultural Revolution, Volume 1: Contradictions Among the People 1956-57 (New York: Columbia University Press, 1974), pp. 205, 290-92. Mao and K'o were photographed together viewing ta-tzu-pao during the Hundred Flowers phase in Shanghai. See China Reconstructs no. 12, December 1957, p. 2; and a reproduction of this photograph in Richard Solomon, Mao's Revolution and the Chinese Political Culture (Berkeley: University of California Press, 1971), p. 306. Solomon agrees with MacFarquhar's analysis of K'o's role during this period, see his Mao's Revolution, pp. 320, 450. K'o's speech on the anti-rightist campaign of 1957 is reprinted in JMJP, 27 August 1957. K'o was additionally elected mayor of Shanghai in November 1958 after Ch'en Yi gave up this post for full-time work in Peking; see SCMP 1900, 14-17.

7. MacFarquhar, Origins, pp. 308-9, 404.

8. Jen-min Jih-pao, 14 June 1957.

9. Lowell Dittmer, Liu Shao-ch'i and the Chinese Cultural Revolution (Berkeley: University of California Press, 1974), p. 186. The article appears in JMJP, 13 October 1958.

10. In a speech at the Lushan Conference in 1960, Mao mentioned K'o Ch'ing-shih and T'an Chen-lin as two who had helped him "shoot the three big cannons" of the Great Leap Forward--the communes, the backyard steel furnaces, and the general line. Byung-joon Ahn, "Adjustments in the Great Leap Forward and Their Ideological Legacy, 1959-62," in Ideology and Politics in Contemporary China, ed. Chalmers Johnson (Seattle: University of Washington Press, 1973), p. 262.

Chapter II Notes

11. K'o's articles defended the principles behind not only the Great
Leap Forward but also the brief 1956 "leap." See JMJP, 25 January 1958, in Current Background 491: 1-34. He also broke
ground in significant new directions that anticipated the later concerns of Chang Ch'un-ch'iao during the Cultural Revolution. K'o's
"The Laboring People Must Make Themselves Masters of Culture"
appeared in the inaugural issue of Hung-ch'i (1 June 1958) under
the direction of Ch'en Po-ta. K'o also analyzed and praised the
campaign for workers to transform technology in Shanghai (see
SCMP 2229; 1960) and as early as 1963 urged that traditional
Chinese dramas be revolutionized to reflect class struggle; see
Hung-ch'i, 15 August 1964. Mao's "Comment on Comrade K'o
Ch'ing-shih's Report," 12 December 1963, was a remark on this
1963 speech on art and culture by K'o, later reprinted in Hung-ch'i.
Mao's remarks are in CB 891. These remarks have been interpreted as a form of pressure by Mao upon Chou Yang to struggle
against dissidents.

Chang himself was a central figure in K'o's efforts to revolutionize literature and art. His article in Shang-hai Wen-hsueh,
January 1960, stressed that Mao's thought should be more strongly
emphasized in literature.

12. CFJP, 9 November 1958; URS Bio 883, 2 June 1964; Who's Who,
pp. 20-21.

13. Merle Goldman, "The Chinese Communist Party's 'Cultural Revolution' of 1962-64," in Ideology and Politics, ed. Johnson, pp. 219-
54, 225-29. Goldman identifies Wu Han, Feng Yu-lan, Liu Chieh,
Yang Han-sheng and Chou Yang in this dissenting category.

14. In 1960 Yao, for example, had been the first writer to label Pa Jen,
a famous 1930's Shanghai literature figure, as a revisionist for his
notion that there was a class-transcending "human nature." See
Pa Jen, "Human Sentiments" URS 19, no. 9 (1960), and "On Collec-
tivism," SCMM 61. Yao also attacked Chou Ku-ch'eng, a Futan
history professor and prominent Marxist of the 1930's, for a mis-
taken conception of dialectical contradiction. See "On Mr. Chou
Ku-ch'eng's Views on Contradiction," JMJP, 18 July 1964, in CB
747: 12-24, and Merle Goldman, "Chinese Communist Party's
'Cultural Revolution'" in Ideology and Politics, ed. Johnson, pp.
230-32.

Chapter II Notes

15. White, "Leadership in Shanghai," pp. 335-36. Pa Chin, a prominent novelist and outspoken anarchist before 1949, had a long history of opposition to CCP policies. As a leading anarchist during the 1920s and '30s, Pa had been an outspoken critic of Communism and historical materialism and was himself often a target of criticism by Chinese Marxists. After 1949, Pa renounced his anarchism, declared his sympathy with the aims of the CCP, and began to participate actively on various cultural committees and friendship delegations. Nevertheless, he continued to be outspoken in his opposition to what he felt to be excessive Party control over cultural life. His frank criticisms of the Party during the Hundred Flowers period turned him into a target during the ensuing anti-rightist campaign in 1957. His public opposition to Yao Wen-yuan in 1962 shows, however, that he continued to be a critic of what he felt to be unjust Party policies and tactics. Pa was eventually branded a counterrevolutionary in February 1968. See Who's Who, p. 533; Howard L. Boorman, ed., Biographical Dictionary of Republican China, vol. II (New York: Columbia University Press, 1967), pp. 297-99; and Olga Lang, Pa Chin and His Writings (Cambridge: Harvard University Press, 1972). Pa's criticism of Yao Wen-yuan's tactics appeared in Shang-hai Wen-hsueh, no. 5 (1962), p. 3; in JPRS 15,515: 15-20.

16. White, "Leadership in Shanghai," pp. 335-37. White's article contains a more comprehensive account of this pivotal pre-Cultural Revolution conflict.

    Shih Hsi-min's support for Ch'en Ch'i-wu's defense of Pa Chin is problematical, since Shih seems to have shared the desire to reform literature and art held by K'o, Chang, and Yao. Shih's article a few years before in Shanghai Chieh-fang ("The New Situation of the Cultural Revolution in Shanghai," Chieh-fang no. 9, 5 May 1960, in SCMM 219: 28-35) called for restricting "bourgeois" culture by propagating a "cultural revolution" in educational work. The key issue here, as during the Cultural Revolution, seems to have been not over whether or not culture needed to be transformed but over what constituted legitimately "bourgeois" influences. Shih apparently thought Yao was off-track.

    It is important to note that Yang Hsi-kuang, who had also supported Pa Chin's position in this dispute, remained as deputy head of the Propaganda Department. This would stir considerable opposition to the Municipal Party Committee by Red Guards

102

Chapter II Notes

during the Cultural Revolution, as Yang became a chief target for attacks after being appointed temporarily to replace Chang Ch'un-ch'iao. See the next chapter of this essay.

17. His appointment as Propaganda chief was announced in CFJP on 3 May and 31 May 1963. His election to the MPC was reported in Hsin-min Wan-pao (New People's Evening News) (HMWP), 30 December 1963.

18. Who's Who, pp. 20-21.

19. That K'o and Mao were cooperating to push for rectification in literary and cultural circles both inside and outside the Party is seen in K'o's previously mentioned speech calling for revolutionization of traditional Chinese drama (reprinted in Hung-ch'i, 15 August 1964) and Mao's favorable comment on it ("Comment on Comrade K'o Ch'ing-shih's Report" 12 December 1963, in CB 891). In this speech and in others, most notably his "Instruction of the Central Committee on Strengthening of Learning from Each Other and Overcoming Conservatism, Arrogance, and Complacency" (13 December 1963, in CB 892) and "Instructions Concerning Literature and Art" (27 June 1964, in CB 891), Mao was putting pressure on Chou Yang to move against dissidents in the national propaganda apparatus.

20. Asia Research Centre, ed., The Great Cultural Revolution in China (Rutland and Tokyo: Charles E. Tuttle, 1968), p. 91.

21. See White, "Shanghai's Polity," in The City in Communist China, ed. Lewis.

22. Donald W. Klein and Anne B. Clark, Biographic Dictionary of Chinese Communism, 1921-1965 (Cambridge: Harvard University Press, 1971), p. 442. As part of the "Dictatorship of the Proletariat" campaign a decade later, K'o Ch'ing-shih's activities were commemorated in a tribute to him by the Shanghai Party's ideological journal. See Yeh Po-lo, "Recalling a Few Things About Comrade K'o Ch'ing-shih" Hsueh-hsi yü p'i-p'an no. 6, 18 June 1975, in Selections from People's Republic of China Magazines 830: 19-34.

23. Yao's piece, originally published in Shanghai's Wen-hui Pao in November, was not reprinted in Peking's Jen-min Jih-pao until

Chapter II Notes

weeks later, at which time a symposium was added, discussing
Yao's positions and defusing the article's effect (see JMJP, 30 November 1965, in CB 783: 1-18). Teng T'o's organ, Pei-ching
Jih-pao, defended Wu Han's play and criticized Yao's November
article (see PCJP, 9 December 1965, in SCMP 3669: 1-5). For
accounts of the infighting and debates touched off by Yao's article
and the subsequent events leading into the Cultural Revolution, see
Goldman, "Chinese Communist Party's 'Cultural Revolution' of
1962-64," in Ideology and Politics, ed. Johnson; Clive Ansley, The
Heresy of Wu Han (Toronto: University of Toronto Press, 1971);
and White, "Shanghai's Polity During the Cultural Revolution," in
The City in Communist China, ed. Lewis.

24. Ch'en and Ts'ao were listed first and second as members of a
55-member presidium preparing for the 5th Municipal People's
Congress; WHP, 30 November 1965, in SCMP(S) 147: 7. Ts'ao's
election at this congress was reported in NCNA Shanghai, 8 December 1965, in SCMP 3599: 1-2.

25. "Retrench the Structure: Send Cadres to Join Labor Production,"
WHP, 6 December 1957; in URS 10: 4-10.

26. The context was a speech to the Rectification Work Committee for
Shanghai's industrial and commercial circles. See Shang-hai
Kung-shang (Shanghai Industry and Commerce), 5 February 1958;
in URS 11: 316-17.

27. See Ts'ao's article in Peking Review, 9 October 1964: 19-22.

28. See WHP, 12 March 1966, in SCMP(S) 151: 24-27, and WHP,
29 April 1966, in SCMP(S) 151: 17-23.

Chapter III Notes

1. Red Guards saw Ch'en's illness as faked and interpreted it as a
sign that he was a genuine capitalist roader all too-aware of what
was in store for him. The "illness" was to provide him with an
escape from criticism and removal, according to this view. (See
Hung-wei Chan-pao [Red Guard Dispatch], 8 January 1967, in
SCMP(S) 166: 9-13 (published jointly by the Red Revolutionaries

Chapter III Notes

and the Shanghai Red Guard Headquarters) and Hung-wei Chan-pao, 10 January 1967, in Hunter, Shanghai Journal, p. 28.)

Whether or not this allegation is correct, Ch'en did at one point use his absence as a shield to fend off criticism. He attended the October Party Work Conference in Peking and, reportedly, made a speech praising Mao's leadership, the Red Guards, and the progress of the Cultural Revolution in Shanghai. But while Liu Shaoch'i, Teng Hsiao-p'ing, and even Mao himself, among others, made self-criticisms, Ch'en could only admit that mistakes had been made in Shanghai too, and that if he hadn't been convalescing from an illness, he probably would have made some of the same mistakes himself. (See Kung-jen Tsao-fan Pao [Workers Rebel News], 10 February 1968, in SCMP 4131: 1-4 (published by the Workers' General Headquarters). For Mao's mild self-criticism, see "Talk at the Central Work Conference" in Chairman Mao Talks to the People, ed. Stuart Schram (New York: Pantheon, 1974), p. 271.

2. Hsin-wen Chan-shih (News Warrior), 26 December 1966, in Hunter, Shanghai Journal, p. 29 (published by the Revolutionary Rebel Committee of Shanghai Press Circles).

3. WHP, 11 June 1966, in URS 44: 100. See also "An Anthology of Wall Posters," (published by the Field Army Red Guards of the Shanghai Foreign Languages Institute) in Hunter, Shanghai Journal, p. 30.

4. WHP, 11 June 1966, in URS 44: 102, and SCMP(S) 153: 2-3.

5. "An Anthology of Wall Posters," in Hunter, Shanghai Journal, pp. 30-31.

We are indebted to the Shanghai Red Guard press for giving us a fairly complex picture of the nonpublic activities of Ts'ao Ti-ch'iu and other MPC members during the period. (The accounts were based on transcripts of meetings and telephone conferences that were subsequently acquired in raids on party offices.) Since these press accounts invariably considered any expression of sympathy for the Cultural Revolution by Ts'ao and others to be a brazen example of "treachery," and since every call for moderation, no matter how mild, was declared to be "an act of white terror," the Red Guards apparently felt little need to edit Ts'ao's comments. The result is, for those who do not share the Red Guard's assumptions, a remarkably balanced account of the complex motives of an embattled man.

Chapter III Notes

6. Chang Ch'un-ch'iao apparently did not vacate his position as Shanghai's Propaganda chief to join the Central Cultural Revolution Group (CCRG) in Peking until late July. Hunter (pp. 139-140) reports that Chang left for Peking to attend the Eleventh Plenum (August 1-12), and after its conclusion stayed in Peking. Chang was repeatedly reported to be in Shanghai and was consistently listed as a member of Shanghai's MPC throughout June (see WHP, 11 June 1966, in URS 44: 97-103, Foreign Broadcast Information Service, Daily Report (Far East) 113, 13 June 1966, ddd. 1-5, and WHP, 1 July 1966: 4.) The first reference to Chang as a member of the CCRG is in "Speech by Comrade Chiang Ch'ing on July 26 at Peking University," in Selections from China Mainland Magazines--Supplement (SCMM(S)), 16: 2. (At the time of this reference it was not yet clear that Chang was in Peking.)

Chang was replaced in Shanghai by Yang Hsi-kuang, who became acting Propaganda chief apparently with the anticipation that Chang would eventually return to his post. This appointment was later taken as a major indication that Ts'ao was a revisionist who was "protecting" Yang, who had found himself on the wrong side of the 1963 literary dispute with Chang Ch'un-ch'iao--the same dispute that led to the elevation of Chang to his present post as head of the Propaganda Department. But Yang, after all, had not been removed by K'o during the earlier dispute, and Yang was probably the next senior Propaganda official at that time, a fairly automatic appointment for such a temporary position. Ts'ao's routine appointment of Yang would later prove to be a major source of Red Guard opposition to the MPC leadership.

7. The proceedings were reported on Shanghai Radio, in FE 2186: B7-10. Chang was among the half-dozen municipal officials in attendance at the speaker's platform.

8. FE 2186: B8; compare these arguments with those made the previous month by Yao Wen-yuan, "On 'Three Family Village'," CFJP, 10 May 1966, in CB 792: 22-44. Ts'ao's above remarks, and those that follow, are patterned closely after Yao's assertions in this article, where he argued that the reactionary line of Wu Han, Teng T'o and Liao Mo-sha had spread throughout the country, requiring that its adherents be rooted out and removed from power before they could engineer a bourgeois restoration.

9. FE 2186: B8-9.

Chapter III Notes

10. FE 2186: B11-13.

11. Parris Chang, "Provincial Party Leaders' Strategies for Survival during the Cultural Revolution," in Elites, ed. Scalapino, pp. 501-39; 506-09. It is important to note that this work team policy was not discredited and abandoned until the 11th Plenum in August, and was official Party policy throughout most of the summer.

12. Who's Who, pp. 229-30.

13. White, "Shanghai's Polity," in Elites, ed. Scalapino, p. 325.

14. WHP, 8 June 1966, in SCMP(S) 153: 5-9. These 1956 pronouncements were used against Ho a full decade later.

15. FE 2185: B18. Merle Goldman's "Party Policies Towards the Intellectuals: The Unique Blooming and Contending of 1961-62," in Party Leadership and Revolutionary Power in China, ed. John Lewis (London: Cambridge University Press, 1970), pp. 268-330, provides an excellent account of the cultural trends during this period, in which Ho was obviously an active participant, as were many others attacked during this summer's rectification campaign.

16. WHP, 8 June 1966; in SCMP(S) 153: 8. See also FE 2185: B17-19.

17. A campaign was apparently orchestrated to have workers and students "settle the score" with Ho by writing letters to municipal newspapers. See WHP, 8 June 1966, in SCMP(S) 153: 5-9, and CFJP, 29 July 1966, in FE 2234: B9.

18. Kuang-ming Jih-pao (KMJP), 4 March 1958; in URS 12: 110-13.

19. See Yao Wen-yuan, "On Mr. Chou Ku-ch'eng's Views on Contradiction," JMJP, 18 July 1964, in CB 747: 12-24. This article had originally appeared in KMJP on 24 September 1963.

20. See Chou Ku-ch'eng, "Unified Whole and Separate Reflections," JMJP, 18 July 1964, in CB 747: 5-11.

21. See WHP, 7 January 1966, in CB 783: 54.

Chapter III Notes

22. See CFJP, 11 August 1966; in SCMP(S) 155: 1-11. There may indeed have been longer-standing scores to settle with Chou Ku-ch'eng held by CCP members. Chou had been a prominent Marxist theoretician of the left-KMT during the 1930s and had participated in theoretical debates with Communists over the proper revolutionary strategy mandated by China's economic conditions. See Arif Dirlik, "National Development and Social Revolution in Early Chinese Marxist Thought," China Quarterly 57 (April-May 1974): 286-309, 294. As a prominent historian, Chou's writings were subject to close scrutiny after 1949 to assure that his accounts corresponded with Party orthodoxy on stages of history. See the references to Chou in A. Feuerwerker and S. Cheng, Chinese Communist Studies of Modern Chinese History (Cambridge: Harvard East Asian Research Center, 1961). Chou was also criticized by Soviet historians, shortly before his purge, for an allegedly "Asia-centric" conception of history. See R. V. Vyatkin and S. L. Tikhvinsky, "Some Questions of Historical Science in the Chinese People's Republic," reprinted in History in Communist China, ed. A. Feuerwerker (Cambridge: MIT Press, 1968), pp. 331-55; 335-38.

23. See Who's Who, pp. 166-67.

24. See the translation of Wu Han's play, along with analysis, in Ansley, The Heresy of Wu Han. The reference to Chou Hsin-fang is on page 4.

25. Who's Who, pp. 166-67, and Ansley, p. 4. The 1959 play was probably produced before themes related to P'eng Teh-huai could be introduced. It is not certain that even the second production of Chou's Hai Jui had such political content.

26. Who's Who, p. 167.

27. See NCNA Shanghai, 14 June 1966, in SCMP 3730: 4-8.

28. See CFJP, 25 June 1966, in FE 2207: B1-4.

29. See WHP, 7 January 1966, in CB 783: 57-58.

30. See CFJP, 25 June 1966, in FE 2201: B3. In Li's case, as in Chou Ku-ch'eng's, there may have been other animosities with CCP

Chapter III Notes

members remaining from before 1949. Li, a CCP member who quit the Party after the suppression of the 1927 Shanghai uprising, later became Chairman of the KMT Kiangsu Provincial Government, where he had reportedly penned a number of anticommunist directives. See Who's Who, p. 374.

31. Chu Pai-yin, director of the Shanghai Film Bureau, for example, spoke out in 1962 for broader portrayal of characters in films and less strict Party censorship. See FE 2191: B9-12. Some, like Li Ping-hsin and Wang Chi-yen, were apparently university professors who simply were frank about their negative feelings toward what they felt were "tyrannous" Party actions in literature and art. See FE 2186: B13. Still others, like Yu Pai and Yu Lo-k'o, were unfortunate enough to have objected to Yao Wen-yuan's criticism of Wu Han. Yu Pai had criticized Yao for his "metaphysical attitude," while Yu Lo-k'o scored him for "mechanical materialism." See WHP, 7 December 1965, in SCMP(S) 148: 1-17; and WHP, 13 February 1966, in SCMP(S) 149: 32-35. While the offense of the latter two was fairly typical of purge victims, we know of no evidence that they were targeted in Shanghai.

32. WHP, 8 June 1966, in SCMP(S) 153: 10-14. The film Ch'en praised had apparently been influenced by the aesthetic ideals of Yang Hsien-chen and others who sought a more realistic portrayal of peasants in films. See Donald Munro, "The Yang Hsien-chen Affair," China Quarterly, April-June 1965; and Goldman, "Party Policies," in Party Leadership, ed. Lewis, pp. 268-303.

33. See MacFarquhar, Origins, Vol. I, pp. 179-80, and Goldman, Literary Dissent, pp. 181-82. MacFarquhar feels that Minister of Defense P'eng Teh-huai, who later indicated disapproval of the liberal Hundred Flowers line, had encouraged and supported Ch'en, since Jen-min Jih-pao was slow to print rebuttals of Ch'en's criticisms. Ch'en was also attacked quite mercilessly by intellectuals in the midst of the Hundred Flowers period; see Roderick MacFarquhar, The Hundred Flowers Campaign and the Chinese Intellectuals (New York: Praeger, 1960), p. 175.

34. Who's Who, p. 78.

35. Shanghai Radio, 22 June 1966, in FE 2207: B7; WHP, 1 June 1966, in URS 44: 173-78; Shanghai Radio, 1 July 1966, in FE 2212: B6.

Chapter III Notes

36. WHP, 7 July and 4 August 1966, in URS 45: 314-19. HMWP, 18 August 1966, in URS 45: 319-27.

37. WHP, 19 May 1966, in SCMP(S) 152: 15-19, HMWP, 21 May 1966, in SCMP(S) 152: 19-20, HMWP, 23 June 1966, in White, "Shanghai's Polity," p. 337.

Chapter IV Notes

1. See Mao Tse-tung, "Speech at the Closing Ceremony of the Eleventh Plenum of the Eighth Central Committee," 12 August 1966, in Chairman Mao, ed. Schram, pp. 262-63, and also Mao, "Interjection at Enlarged Meeting of the CCPCC Standing Committee," 4 August 1966, in Miscellany of Mao Tse-tung Thought, JPRS 49, 826: 16-18.

2. As other Red Guard Headquarters were later formed with the intention of "dragging out" the leaders of the MPC, this original federation became known as the "First Headquarters," see Hunter, Shanghai Journal, p. 83.

3. Shanghai correspondent for Far Eastern Economic Review (FEER), 8 September 1966, in China News Items from the Press (CNI), no. 136.

4. WHP, 20 August 1966, in SCMP(S) 156: 29-33. Ts'ao led a parade throughout the city after the rally, at which Kuo Mo-jo gave a speech. See NCNA Shanghai, 19 August 1966, in FE 2245: B2-3. Chang was by this time in Peking with the Cultural Revolution Group. He appeared on the rostrum at a Tienanmen rally that same week. See Peking Radio, 10 August 1966, in FE 2243: B1-2; and FE 2244: B3-4.

5. Hsin-wen Chan-shih, 26 December 1966, in Hunter, Shanghai Journal, p. 36.

6. Shanghai Radio, 24 August 1966, in FE 2252: B3; Shanghai Radio, 14 September 1966, in FE 2268: B5-6; and Shanghai Radio, 16 October 1966, in FE 2294: B1.

7. CFJP, 22 August 1966, in URS 52: 345-46.

Chapter IV Notes

8. See Shanghai correspondent reports from FEER, 8 September 1966, in CNI 136; South China Morning Post (Hong Kong), 8 September 1966, in CNI 137; and South China Morning Post, 24 August 1966, in CNI 139.

9. See Shanghai correspondent reports from South China Morning Post, 23 August and 8 September 1966, in CNI 137.

10. See South China Morning Post, 8 September and 14 September 1966, in CNI 137; and South China Morning Post, 27 September 1966, in CNI 139.

11. See, for example, Shanghai Radio, 14 September 1966, in FE 2268: B5-6; Shanghai Radio, 30 September 1966, in FE 2284: B7; and South China Morning Post, 27 September 1966, in CNI 139.

12. This was, at that time, a matter of Party policy. Those initially excluded did not belong to a family in one of the "five red categories"--workers, poor and lower-middle peasants, cadres, armymen, and martyrs. Hong Yung Lee has recently argued that these excluded students had a strong incentive to push their criticisms of authority much further than others were willing. See his excellent discussion of "The Behavior of the Radicals" (pp. 655-63) and "The Social Characteristics of the Student Radicals" (pp. 673-81) in Hong Yung Lee, "The Radical Students in Kwangtung During the Cultural Revolution," China Quarterly 64 (December 1975): 645-83.

13. Student demands on this count often required the school Party Committee to break existing CCRG directives relating to confidential files and secret materials, and student actions in storming the offices containing the "black material" clearly defied CCRG policy on archives and secret files. See Hunter, Shanghai Journal, pp. 111-31, and the relevant CCP Documents in CB 852: 16, 24-25.
    The position of the Party Committee at Shanghai Foreign Languages Institute was made even more complicated by the fact that they had never labelled anyone counterrevolutionary, nor forced anyone to make a confession. For that reason it was quite likely, Hunter feels, that the "black material" did not exist at the Institute. See Hunter, Shanghai Journal, pp. 118-22.

Chapter IV Notes

14. Hung-wei Chan-pao, 15 November 1966, in Hunter, Shanghai
    Journal, p. 84. The August 22 speech was probably similar in
    tone to his above cited speech (footnote 28) which appeared in WHP
    on August 20. The "Sixteen Points" had been adopted during the
    August Plenum only two weeks before and were considered the
    "charter" of the Red Guard movement and a guide to behavior for
    both leaders and masses. See CCP Documents of the Great Prole-
    tarian Cultural Revolution (CCP Documents) (Hong Kong: Union
    Research Institute, 1968), pp. 42-54. An examination of this
    document reveals that Ts'ao was being extremely careful, in both
    word and deed, to stick carefully to its provisions. This would
    come to characterize his dealings with the student and worker
    dissident movements.

15. Hunter, Shanghai Journal, p. 84.

16. Hung-wei Chan-pao, 15 November 1966, in Hunter, Shanghai
    Journal, p. 85. This apparently coincided with the rally of Peking
    students described below.

17. Hung-wei Chan-pao, 15 November 1966, in Hunter, Shanghai
    Journal, p. 83.

18. Hung-wei Chan-pao, 15 November 1966, in Hunter, Shanghai
    Journal, p. 83. It emerged again as a central concern of the city
    leadership in February and March 1967, as a whole array of dis-
    sident groups, who considered themselves "true revolutionary
    leftists" and Chang Ch'un-ch'iao an "opportunist" and "revisionist,"
    protested against their exclusion from basic level "great alliances."
    Chang's reaction, unlike Ts'ao's, was to brand these groups
    "counterrevolutionaries."

19. See WHP, CFJP, and Shanghai Radio, 28 August 1966, in FE
    2253: B9-10. The Peking media also provided coverage of the
    Tibetan students' actions; see NCNA Peking, 28 August 1966; in
    FE 2252: B3-4. As if to draw a moral lesson from this episode,
    Jen-min Jih-pao ran an editorial on the 28th entitled "Revolutionary
    Young People Should Learn from the Chinese People's Liberation
    Army."

Chapter IV Notes

20. Nieh Yuan-tzu was a philosophy professor and a leader of the militant Red Guard factions in Peking that had advocated attacks on the Party apparatus. Nieh's earlier poster was reprinted in People's Daily on the order of Chairman Mao. It was rumored that Ts'ao Ti-ch'iu had seen these attacks on the Shanghai Party while in Peking for the Eleventh Plenum. See Hung-wei Chan-pao, 15 November 1966, in Hunter, Shanghai Journal, p. 80, and Hung-wei Chan-pao, 8 January 1967, in SCMP(S) 166: 14-15. If this were the case, it no doubt alerted Ts'ao to the threat of the Peking Red Guards and the necessity for him to stick closely to established directives and not make any errors.

21. Chang was often reported as one of several Cultural Revolution Group officials who appeared jointly at Red Guard meetings. On at least one occasion, later that autumn, Chang was reported to hold a personal conference with Red Guards on political work methods. See Peking Radio, 11 November 1966, in FE·2316: B2, and SCMM(S) 16: 23-24.

22. Shanghai Radio, 26 August 1966, in FE 2252: B2.

23. Hsin-wen Chan-shih, 26 December 1966, in Hunter, Shanghai Journal, p. 91.

24. Shanghai Radio, 28 August 1966, in FE 2253: B9-10; and Hung-wei Chan-pao, 15 November 1966, in Hunter, Shanghai Journal, pp. 91-92.

25. See Shanghai correspondent for Hong Kong Kuai Pao, 16 September 1966, in CNI 138, pp. 9-10, and Hunter, Shanghai Journal, pp. 96, 109.

26. For the former account, see Hunter, Shanghai Journal, pp. 97-98; for the latter, see leaflets signed by "The Revolutionary Workers and Employees" of "Shanghai's largest textile factory," which denounced the occupation and demanded immediate withdrawal, in South China Morning Post, 13 September 1966, in CNI 137.

27. Hung-wei Chan-pao, 8 January 1967, in SCMP(S) 166: 15.

28. Hung-wei Chan-pao, 15 November 1966, in Hunter, Shanghai Journal, p. 98.

Chapter IV Notes

29. Hunter, Shanghai Journal, pp. 99-100.

30. Shanghai Radio, 5 September 1966, in FE 2266: B2-3.

31. Hung-wei Chan-pao, 15 November 1966, in Hunter, Shanghai Journal, p. 98.

32. Hung-wei Chan-pao, 30 December 1966, in Hunter, Shanghai Journal, pp. 94-95. Mao expressed identical reservations about the intellectual and political content of Red Guard slogans and about the practice of "bringing everyone down." His conclusion, in February 1967, was that the orientation of this sector of the Red Guard movement was indeed in error and was in fact reactionary. See Mao, "Talks at Three Meetings with Comrades Chang Ch'un-ch'iao and Yao Wen-yuan," in Chairman Mao, ed. Schram, p. 277.

33. Although certainly not an accurate generalization for the movement as a whole, Yang's observation, if the experience of the Canton Red Guard Dai Hsiao-ai is any guide, certainly describes the actions of a significant portion of the movement. See Gordon Bennett and Ronald Montaperto, Red Guard: The Political Biography of Dai Hsiao-ai (Garden City, New York: Doubleday, 1972), pp. 107-25.

34. Hung-wei Chan-pao, 8 January 1967, in SCMP(S) 166: 15.

35. Ibid., p. 15.

36. Ibid., p. 17. This observation seems like little more than a weak attempt to discredit the MPC's opposition, but there are strong indications that it was an accurate one. Mao himself admitted a few weeks later at the October Work Conference that "some of the students did not have terribly good family background . . ." (Schram, p. 268), and Chang Ch'un-ch'iao would later label the orientation of these same student groups as "petit bourgeois" when they opposed his administration. Hong Yung Lee's thorough research also points in this direction. See his "Radical Students in Kwangtung," pp. 673-77, where he argues that the "radicals" in the student movement were very often of bourgeois family background.

Chapter IV Notes

37. Hung-wei Chan-pao, 30 December 1966, in Hunter, Shanghai Journal, pp. 94-95.

38. Hung-wei Chan-pao, 8 January 1967, in SCMP(S) 166: 15.

39. Hsin-wen Chan-shih, 26 December 1966, in Hunter, Shanghai Journal, p. 36.

40. Hung-wei Chan-pao, 30 December 1966, in Hunter, Shanghai Journal, p. 36. These attempts by Yang to "set the tone" were later major accusations made against him by dissident Red Guards, who accused him of diverting the spearhead of struggle away from the handful of revisionist leaders.

41. See, for example, Shanghai Radio, 30 September 1966, in FE 2285: B6-7; WHP, 2 October 1966, in SCMP(S) 158: 17-20; South China Morning Post, 21 October 1966, in CNI 143; and Hunter, Shanghai Journal, p. 109.

42. Hunter, Shanghai Journal, p. 110.

43. Hung-wei Chan-pao, 8 January 1967, in SCMP(S) 166: 16.

44. 8-25 October 1966.

45. Mao, "Talk at the Report Meeting," 24 October 1966, in Chairman Mao, ed. Schram, p. 264.

46. Mao, Ibid., p. 264. Mao would prove wrong in this assertion. P'an Fu-sheng, first party secretary of Helungkiang, was later hospitalized after following Mao's advice. Wan Hsiao-tung, first secretary of Tientsin, reportedly died as a result of the treatment he received at a struggle meeting with students. See P. Chang, "Provincial Leaders," in Elites, ed. Scalapino, p. 510. Ts'ao apparently had good reason to keep his distance from large groups of dissident students.

47. Mao, "Talk at the Report Meeting," 24 October 1966, in Chairman Mao, ed. Schram, p. 264.

Chapter IV Notes

48. Mao, "Talk at the Central Work Conference," 25 October 1966, in Chairman Mao, ed. Schram, p. 271. See the same confession in "Talk at the Report Meeting," 24 October 1966, Ibid., p. 265.

49. Mao, "Talk at the Central Work Conference," 25 October 1966, Ibid., p. 272.

50. Ibid., and Mao, "Talk at the Report Meeting," 24 October 1966, Ibid., p. 264.

51. Mao, "Talk at the Central Work Conference," 25 October 1966, Ibid., p. 273.

52. Ibid., p. 272.

53. It is safe to assume that Ts'ao attended the October Conference since it was of such vital importance and since he did not appear in Shanghai media accounts during the period.

Chapter V Notes

1. See point 14 of the "Sixteen Points" in CCP Documents, pp. 42-54.

2. Jen-min Jih-pao editorial entitled "Taking a Firm Hold on the Revolution and Stimulating Production is a Policy of Mao," broadcast over Shanghai Radio, 10 November 1966, in FE 2314: B3.

3. See, for example, the account by a detachment from Peking Aeronautical Institute that tried to establish a liaison at the No. 1 Machine Tool Factory, in Hung-ch'i no. 2, 16 January 1967, in JPRS 40,041: 53-57. This account attributed friction to "arrogant and dictatorial" student work-styles and fear by workers that the students would damage machines and loot the unit's files. This led to brawls and walkouts. See also "Main Points of Conversation Between Comrades Chang Ch'un-ch'iao and Ch'i Pen-yu and Five Fighters of the 'Red Flag' Combat Team of Peking Aeronautical Institute," in SCMM(S) 16: 23-24, and also Hunter, Shanghai Journal, p. 105.

Chapter V Notes

4. See JMJP, 7 September 1966, in CNI 138, p. 2, where Red Guards were warned to "grasp revolution and stimulate production" and not to interfere with work in factories and communes. See similar warnings in JMJP, 15 September 1966, in CNI 138, p. 7; and also Nihon Kezai, Sankei, and Mainichi, 16 September 1966, in Daily Summary of the Japanese Press (DSJP), 16 September 1966, pp. 12, 16, and 22; and Asahi, 7 September 1966, in DSJP, 8 September 1966, p. 28.

5. Tokyo Shimbun, 16 September 1966, in DSJP, 16 September 1966, pp. 11-12.

6. Hung-wei Chan-pao, 8 January 1967, in SCMP(S) 166: 16.

7. See, for example, the efforts of Chang Ch'un-ch'iao to communicate this to "Red Flag" fighters from Peking Aeronautical, in SCMM(S) 16: 23-24.

8. Japanese correspondents relayed a series of Peking wall posters stating that the CCP policy discouraged workers' organizations, and learned through interviews with plant Party Committee members that the current Central policy was for workers to join militia units instead of Red Guard-type organizations. See Tokyo Shimbun, 5 November 1966, and Nihon Kezai, 5 November 1966, in DSJP, 5 November 1966, pp. 22-23; Mainichi, 5 November 1966, in DSJP, 8 November 1966, pp. 9-10; and Hunter, Shanghai Journal, pp. 132-33, 136.

9. Arguments and evidence for the social composition of these dissident workers will be presented in the next section on the social origins of economism.

10. Hung-wei Chan-pao, 8 January 1966, in SCMP(S) 166: 20-21, and Hunter, Shanghai Journal, pp. 137-38.

11. Hung-se Tsao-fan Pao (Red Rebel News), 28 February 1967 (Published by the Shanghai Liaison Center of the Red Rebel Brigade from Harbin Military Engineering Institute), in Hunter, Shanghai Journal, pp. 136-37, CFJP, 8 November 1966, and Shanghai Radio, 8 November 1966, in FE 2319: B21; WHP, 9 November and 10 November 1966, in SCMP(S) 159: 6-20, and Shanghai Radio, 10 November 1966, in FE 2314: B3.

Chapter V Notes

12.   <u>FE</u> 2314: B3.

13.   <u>Hung-wei Chan-pao</u>, 8 January 1967, in <u>SCMP(S)</u> 166: 20-21, and Hunter, <u>Shanghai Journal</u>, p. 138. It is possible that in drawing up additional demands, the leaders of the workers, perhaps influenced by Peking Red Guards, were hoping to ensure rejection and maintain the confrontation with municipal officials.

14.   <u>Hung-wei Chan-pao</u>, 8 January 1967, in <u>SCMP(S)</u> 166: 20-22, and Hunter, <u>Shanghai Journal</u>, p. 139.

15.   <u>Hung-wei Chan-pao</u>, 8 January 1967, in <u>SCMP(S)</u> 166: 21-22. The text of the telegram was copied by Neale Hunter from a Shanghai wall poster; see Hunter, <u>Shanghai Journal</u>, pp. 139-40.

16.   This time sequence is crucial in interpreting the events at Anting. For some reason Hunter claims that there was a "serious split in the Mao group." He asserts that Chang Ch'un-ch'iao literally raced to Shanghai in an attempt to forestall the reading of Ch'en's telegram to the workers and sign the demands before it could be read (pp. 140-41). Hunter interprets this to mean that Chang felt, even more strongly than Ch'en Po-ta, that the workers' demands be recognized. However, Ch'en's telegram could have reached the workers on the 10th, 11th, or even early on the 12th before Chang arrived in Shanghai that day. This possibility is not considered by Hunter, but it makes an entirely different interpretation equally likely--one, incidentally, that fits with other events associated with the "incident." Ch'en's telegram, in this alternative interpretation, <u>was</u> read to the workers, and when this failed to move over half of them, only then was Chang--who as a Shanghai Party official would have been a logical choice--dispatched to negotiate with the workers in order to get them to return to work. This alternative interpretation takes into account the three-day time period that the workers stayed at Anting, and is verified by Hunter's own admission that a brigade of workers left Anting for Peking in order to protest Ch'en's "repressive" telegram. (See <u>Kung-jen Tsao-fan Pao</u>, 13 March 1967, in Hunter, <u>Shanghai Journal</u>, p. 143). This explanation does not require us to imagine that Chang, a vice-director of the CCRG, would defy its director, Ch'en Po-ta. The two leaders of the CCRG were probably in far greater agreement over this crucial issue than other accounts would have it.

Chapter V Notes

17. Chang probably reached Shanghai no sooner than the 12th. On the 10th he was reported to be on the rostrum at a mass rally at Tienanmen Square (see JMJP, 12 November 1966, p. 1, and Peking Radio, 10 November 1966, in FE 2314: B3, and on the 11th he attended another Tienanmen rally and held a conference with Red Guards from Peking Aeronautical Institute. (See Peking Radio, 11 November 1966, in FE 2316: B2; and SCMM(S) 16: 23-24.)

18. Tannenbaum, "The 1967 January Revolution Recounted," p. 15.

19. See Hung-wei Chan-pao, 8 January 1967, in SCMP(S) 166: 20-22, and Hunter, Shanghai Journal, p. 142.

20. Hunter, Shanghai Journal, p. 141.

21. Hung-wei Chan-pao, 8 January 1967, in SCMP(S) 166: 22-23.

22. Ibid., pp. 22-23, and Kung-jen Tsao-fan Pao, 13 March 1967, in Hunter, Shanghai Journal, pp. 143, 224. Keng Chin-chang's brigade would gradually grow into a huge workers' organization known as the Second Regiment, which would challenge Chang's leadership in January and February.

23. CCP Documents, pp. 116-19.

24. This was one of the second set of demands that the Workers' Headquarters had forwarded as a condition for their return to work--the local Party apparatus had to accept blame for the incident. Chang, in signing this demand, had accepted the blame for the Shanghai Party apparatus without even consulting its members. See Hung-wei Chan-pao, 8 January 1967, in SCMP(S) 166: 7-8.

25. Hsin-wen Chan-pao, 26 December 1966, and Hung-wei Chan-pao, 30 December 1966, in Hunter, Shanghai Journal, pp. 144-45.

26. Hung-wei Chan-pao, 8 January 1967, in SCMP(S) 166: 7-8, and Hunter, Shanghai Journal, pp. 144-45.

27. Hung-wei Chan-pao, 8 January 1967, in SCMP(S) 166: 8.

28. Hsin-wen Chan-shih, 26 December 1966, in Hunter, Shanghai Journal, p. 145.

Chapter V Notes

29. Hung-wei Chan-pao, 8 January 1967, in SCMP(S) 166: 8.

30. Hung-wei Chan-pao, 30 December 1966, in Hunter, Shanghai Journal, p. 144. These warnings, which had little effect on CCRG policy towards workers' organizations, were eventually to prove to be correct. The MPC would later be held responsible for the fulfillment of their prophecy. As CCRG officials later grappled with the severe dislocations caused by ignoring these warnings, MPC protestations that workers' organizations would eventually paralyze production were held up as prima facie evidence that the former local officials had opposed the Cultural Revolution.

31. Hung-wei Chan-pao, 8 January 1967, in SCMP(S) 166: 8.

32. Ibid., pp. 21-22. Yu Ch'iu-li was listed in Red Guard materials as a party secretary from Shensi Province--but the dissident students had apparently not been keeping up in their reading. Yu had been appointed the previous November as vice-chairman of the State Planning Commission, and held a simultaneous position as minister of the Petroleum Industry. See NCNA Peking 28 November 1965, in SCMP 3590, p. 1.

33. Ibid., p. 18.

34. CCP Documents, pp. 133-35.

35. Hung-wei Chan-pao, 17 December 1966, in Hunter, Shanghai Journal, pp. 152-55.

36. Ibid., in Hunter, p. 156.

37. Ibid., in Hunter, pp. 157-58.

38. The Scarlet Guards were officially known as "Worker Scarlet Guards for the Defense of Mao Tse-tung's Thought," which later often appeared in translations as "Red Militia Detachment" and "Red Defense Corps," probably as a result of one of the name changes referred to by Hunter in Shanghai Journal, pp. 185-86. For detailed accounts of this week-long affair, see Hong Kong's Sing Tao Daily, 5 March 1967, in CNI 160, p. 9; and Hunter, Shanghai Journal, pp. 159-65.

Chapter V Notes

39. See Hunter, Shanghai Journal, pp. 166–69, and Sophia Knight, Window on Shanghai: Letters from China 1965–67 (London: Andre Deutsch, 1967), p. 236.

40. See, for example, Shanghai Radio, 5 December 1966, in FE 2338: B7.

41. Hsin-wen Chan-shih, 26 December 1966, in Hunter, Shanghai Journal, p. 167.

42. Hung-wei Chan-pao, 30 December 1966, in Hunter, Shanghai Journal, pp. 166–67.

43. Hunter, Shanghai Journal, p. 174.

44. Copied from a wall poster, Hunter, Shanghai Journal, pp. 168–69.

45. Ko-ming Tsao-fan Pao, 15 December 1966 (published by the Revolutionary Rebel Headquarters of Shanghai Red Guards), in Hunter, Shanghai Journal, p. 181.

46. Hung-wei Chan-pao, 30 December 1966, in Hunter, Shanghai Journal, pp. 173–74.

47. Hung-wei Chan-pao, 10 January 1967, in Hunter, Shanghai Journal, pp. 181–82.

48. For example, an "armed clash" occurred in No. 24 Sechih Mill between Scarlets and Rebels, an example of the sort of violence that had become "city-wide" in character. See WHP, 24 December 1967, in SCMP(S) 220: 11.

49. Hunter, Shanghai Journal, p. 177.

50. Hsin-wen Chan-shih, 26 December 1966, Ibid., pp. 186–88.

51. Hung-wei Chan-pao, 4 January 1967, Ibid., p. 189.

52. Hung-wei Chan-pao, 10 January 1967, Ibid., p. 191.

53. Canton Ta-p'i-p'an T'ung-hsun (Mass Criticism and Repudiation Bulletin), 5 October 1967, in SCMP 4125: 5–6.

Chapter V Notes

54. Hung-wei Chan-pao, 8 January 1967, in SCMP(S) 166: 5-9, and Hunter, Shanghai Journal, pp. 197-202.

55. See Hunter, Shanghai Journal, p. 202.

Chapter VI Notes

1. See, for example, WHP, 5 January 1967, in FE 2359: B1-2.

2. See, for example, Jean Esmein, The Chinese Cultural Revolution (New York: Anchor-Doubleday, 1973), p. 181. Esmein feels that this was a spontaneous effort by managers to "buy popularity." K. S. Karol forwards a similar interpretation in The Second Chinese Revolution, p. 215.

3. See, for example, Tannenbaum, "The 1967 January Revolution Recounted," pp. 21-22; Hunter, Shanghai Journal, p. 216, Daubier, History of the Chinese Cultural Revolution, p. 125, and Nee, "Revolution and Bureaucracy," pp. 331-32, all of whom uncritically accept the later assertion that the handouts were a planned strategy by top MPC leaders to direct struggle away from themselves and discredit the Cultural Revolution. Lynn White seems recently to have tentatively embraced a corollary of this view. In his recent "Local Autonomy in China During the Cultural Revolution" (American Political Science Review 70 (June 1976): 483), White presents the payments to workers during late December and early January as an example of the exercise of "local autonomy" by "rightists" in the MPC. And in Parris Chang's scenario for the Cultural Revolution in China as a whole, payoffs by provincial leaders to local rebels are seen as a defensive attempt to coopt opposition. P. Chang presumably has Shanghai, the best known presumed example of this, in mind. See his "Provincial Party Leaders' Strategies," in Elites, ed. Scalapino, pp. 501-39; 524-25.

4. See "Sources of Labor Discontent in China: The Worker-Peasant System," Current Scene (CS) 6 (15 March 1968): 7-12.

5. Permanent laborers work full time, are usually skilled, and are eligible for union health and welfare benefits. Contract laborers usually include semiskilled or apprentice workers. Contracts

Chapter VI Notes

are definite, long-term, and relatively enforceable, but this category is ineligible for the range of benefits enjoyed by permanent workers. Temporary labor is short-term work done without benefit of a contract. This category receives little besides a wage, and can be terminated at any time.

Contract laborers usually came from the suburban communes near Shanghai. Upon termination of the contract, workers returned to the commune, contributing a fixed proportion of their wages to collective funds. They were an integral part of the worker-peasant system. Temporary labor, while not an integral part of the worker-peasant system, increased in importance along with the general de-emphasis on permanent labor. Temporary laborers were usually unemployed peasants who had migrated to Shanghai in the early 1960s or middle school graduates who could neither find permanent jobs nor gain entrance to college, and who resisted being sent to border regions for labor. Labor stations set up in Shanghai neighborhoods became contractors for these marginally employed and suppliers of short-term labor for industry. See Lynn T. White III "Workers Politics in Shanghai," Journal of Asian Studies 36 (November 1976): 99-116, 99-101.

6. See Ibid., pp. 111-16, and CS 6 (15 March 1968): 7-12.

7. WHP, 26 September 1964, quoted in White, "Workers Politics," p. 111.

8. See NCNA Ch'engtu, 27 December 1965, in SCMP 3615: 18-20.

9. Ibid., p. 18.

10. See Kung-jen Jih-pao, 27 April 1966, in SCMP 3693: 6-9, and NCNA Peking, 27 December 1965, in SCMP 3615: 16-18.

11. JMJP, 8 January 1966, in SCMP 3624: 14-18.

12. NCNA Peking, 27 December 1965; in SCMP 3615: 17.

13. See Lynn T. White III, "The Contract Proletariat," mimeographed (Hong Kong: Centre of Asian Studies, The University of Hong Kong, 1972), pp. 39-41.

Chapter VI Notes

14. CFJP, 5 May 1966, in SCMP(S) 154: 11-13, and Shanghai Radio, in FE 2277: B14.

15. WHP, 19 May 1966, in SCMP(S) 152: 15-17, and CFJP, 19 May 1966, in SCMP(S) 154: 13-14.

16. Identical reasons were to be forwarded under Chang Ch'un-ch'iao in 1967 for students to return to the countryside posts they had left. See WHP, 19 May 1966, in SCMP(S) 152: 15-17.

17. See WHP, 19 May 1966, in SCMP(S) 152: 17-19; HMWP, 21 May 1966, in SCMP(S) 152: 19-20; CFJP, 5 May 1966, in SCMP(S) 154: 11-13; and Urumchi Radio, 24 September 1966, in FE 227: B14.

18. Hunter, "Port in a Storm," FEER 56;12; pp. 663-67.

19. Ibid., p. 664.

20. See White, "Workers Politics," pp. 114-15.

21. Hunter, "Port in a Storm," p. 664.

22. See Ke-ming Lou (Revolutionary Tower), 10 March 1967 (Published by Rebels from Shanghai Drama Institute), in SCMP(S) 182: 14-21; and WHP, 11 March 1967, in SCMP 3902: 19-20. Another group that surfaced in Shanghai during the period, yet which does not fit into the socioeconomic trends we are outlining here are the "demobilized soldiers." These were PLA troops who had been transferred to frontier outposts to reclaim land. Some of these groups travelled to Shanghai and proved to be formidable street fighters during January and February of 1967. See P. Chang, "Provincial Party Leaders," p. 523.

23. Hunter, "Port in a Storm," p. 664. White explores these and other differences between the student-technician apprentices and apprentice workers in his "The Contract Proletariat," pp. 39-41.

24. Karol, Second Chinese Revolution, p. 237.

25. Hung Ch'i 2, 16 January 1967, in JPRS 40,041: 43-44.

Chapter VI Notes

26. WHP, 25 January 1967, in URS 47: 174-76.

27. See Ibid., 174-76, and WHP, 7 March 1967, in SCMP(S) 176: 21-22.

28. Leaflet, "Another Message to the People of Shanghai," in Hunter, Shanghai Journal, p. 205.

29. WHP, 12 February 1967, in SCMP 167: 32.

30. Ray Wylie, "Red Guards Rebound," FEER 52;10; pp. 462-67. See also Hunter, Shanghai Journal, p. 220.

31. It is quite likely that this group was most unhappy about fellow commune members who were employed in the city as contract or temporary labor. While contract labor was disadvantaged relative to the permanent labor force, it received greater cash remuneration than did commune laborers. See Wylie, "Red Guards Rebound," pp. 462-67, and WHP, 20 January 1967, in China News Analysis (CNA) 647: 4-5.

32. These are just some of the charges made and demands forwarded by an organization of temporary and contract laborers in Shanghai. See Hung-kung Chan-pao (Red Worker Combat News), 6 February 1967, in SCMP(S) 177: 18-22. The difference in material benefits between this sector and the permanent labor force was indeed great. See White, "Workers Politics," pp. 108-14.

33. See Shanghai Radio, 2 March 1967, in FE 2408: B1.

34. See WHP, 6 January 1967, and Shanghai Radio, 5 January 1967, in FE 2359: B3, which indicate that the temporary workers' organizations were supported by the Rebel faction at that time (this support, incidentally, would wane as Chang Ch'un-ch'iao assumed control over the Workers' Headquarters). See also Ray Wylie, "Red Guards Rebound," p. 465.

35. See Shanghai Radio, 2 March 1967, in FE 2408: B1.

36. See Michel Oksenberg, "Occupational Groups in Chinese Society and the Cultural Revolution," in The Cultural Revolution: 1967 in

Chapter VI Notes

Review (Ann Arbor, Michigan: Center for Chinese Studies, 1968), pp. 1-44, 8-12. Oksenberg's discussion lays out a framework for understanding any perceived alliances between managers, union officials, and permanent workers on the one hand and cleavages between permanent and contract labor on the other as a product of the way benefits were structured and group interests shaped.

37. See Hunter, Shanghai Journal, pp. 166-69, and chapter V above, where the Scarlets, at first, scrupulously held rallies after working hours.

38. See Shanghai Radio, 7 March 1967, in FE 2412: B24, and Asahi, 22 February 1967, in DSJP, 1 March 1967, pp. 25-27.

39. See Shanghai Radio, 23 January 1967, in FE 2375: B9-10, and WHP, 24 January 1967, in CNA 653: 1-2.

40. Asahi, 22 February 1967, in DSJP, 1 March 1967, pp. 25-27.

41. See Japanese visitors' reports in Nihon Kezai, 15 January 1967, in DSJP, 14-16 January 1967, p. 18; and Asahi, 22 February 1967, in DSJP, 1 March 1967, pp. 25-27.

42. See CNA 645: 5-6.

43. See the Central directive addressing this problem in SCMM(S) 17: 14-15.

44. See NCNA Shanghai, 24 January 1967, in FE 2377: B5-6; WHP, 22 January 1967, in CNA 649: 4; WHP, 29 March 1967, in FE 2430: B8-9; and Asahi, 22 February 1967, in DSJP, 1 March 1967, pp. 25-27.

45. See Shanghai Radio, 2 March 1967, in FE 2408: B1, and Hung-kung Chan-pao, 6 February 1967, in SCMP(S) 177: 18-22.

46. From Canton wall-posters, dated 4 January 1967, cited in Current Scene, 15 March 1968, p. 9. A text of Chiang Ch'ing's meeting with workers is in Chung Hua-min and Arthur Miller, Madame Mao: A Profile of Chiang Ch'ing (Hong Kong: Union Research Institute, 1968).

Chapter VI Notes

47. See JMJP, 26 December 1966, in SCMP 3852: 1; Current Scene,
     15 March 1968, p. 8; and Asahi, 12 January 1967, in CNA 644: 3.

48. Current Scene, 15 March 1968, p. 9.

49. Shanghai Radio, 2 March 1967, in FE 2408: B1. This was a
     Workers' Headquarters order repudiating the agreement, and it
     coincided with the second lay-off of these workers and the disband-
     ment of their organizations.

50. See the accounts by a worker from the Shanghai Electric Bulb
     Factory, and by a detachment of the Shanghai Chingkangshan
     Liaison Station, in Hung-ch'i 2, 16 January 1967, in JPRS 40,041,
     pp. 41-42.

51. See the accusations in CFJP, 10 January 1967, in FE 2363: B6-8.

52. See, for example, the experience at Shanghai's docks, in Hunter,
     "Port in a Storm," p. 664.

53. See the 1967 interview with three members of Shanghai's Revolu-
     tionary Committee by Manlio Dinucci, in Nuova Unita, organ of
     the Communist Party (Marxist-Leninist) of Italy, July-August
     1967, in JPRS 42,525, pp. 1-24, 8; Wylie, "Red Guards Rebound,"
     p. 464; and WHP, 20 January 1967, in CNA 647: 4-5.

54. Hunter, Shanghai Journal, pp. 196-97, estimates the number of
     departing Scarlets at sixty to seventy thousand. JMJP, 23 Janu-
     ary 1967, in SCMP 3869: 1-3, reveals that most of the workers
     demanding travel expenses at that time were from "Red Militia
     Detachments" (Scarlet Guards).

55. See Bennett and Montaperto, Red Guard, pp. 118-19.

56. See, for example, the account from the "Publications Bureau
     Printing Corporation," in WHP, 22 January 1967, in URS 46:
     341-44, and SCMP(S) 169: 27-29.

57. WHP, 19 January 1967, in SCMP 3876: 8-10. This estimate for
     the Scarlets' numerical strength is almost universally quoted by
     both factions. See the leaflet "Urgent Appeal" 31 December 1966

Chapter VI Notes

(Published by the Scarlet Guards), in Hunter, Shanghai Journal, p. 194; Nuova Unita in JPRS 42,525, p. 8; Asahi, 13 May 1967, in DSJP, 18 May 1967, p. 15; and Chang Ch'un-ch'iao, in URS 50: 18.

58. See WHP, 19 January 1967, in SCMP 3876: 8-11. The "Editor's Note" accompanying these articles nonetheless asserted that these documents proved complicity on the part of the "small handful" in the Scarlet and MPC leadership.

59. Since the force of Scarlets leaving Shanghai was between sixty and seventy thousand, it would have required a force of almost equal size to turn them back at Kunshan.

60. NCNA, 19 January 1967, in FE 2370: B24-25. Manlio Dinucci was told that in one small neighborhood clock factory alone, 10,540 yuan of back pay and wages were withdrawn from the factory's operating funds. See Nuova Unita in JPRS 42,525, p. 15.

61. JMJP, 21 January 1967, in URS 46: 207, and NCNA, 19 January 1967, in FE 2370: B24-25. See reports from Peking of similar, though less serious occurrences, apparently touched off by the official order to release factory funds, in Czechoslovak Press Service, 8 January 1967, in FE 2370: C3.

62. See NCNA, 9 February 1967, in FE 2389: B33; Peking Radio, 16 January 1967, in FE 2368: B19; and Asahi, 7 January 1967, in CNA 651: 1-2. For a detailed account see White, "Shanghai's Polity," pp. 328-30.

63. See South China Morning Post, 1 February 1967, in CNI 156; Peking Radio, 16 January 1967, in FE 2368: B19; Nuova Unita in JPRS 42,525, p. 9; and Hung-ch'i 10, 9 August 1967, pp. 36-40 (Reprint of articles from Shanghai Hai-kang Chan-pao--The Harbor Warrior), in White, "Shanghai's Polity," p. 329.

64. See NCNA, 16 January 1967, in SCMP 3864, pp. 20-21; and FE 2370: B14-17; Peking Radio, 8 February 1967, in FE 2390: B19; and White, "Shanghai's Polity," p. 329.

65. JMJP, 21 February 1967, in CNA 654: 6; and Shanghai Radio, 20 February 1967, in FE 2399: B21-22.

Chapter VI Notes

66. WHP, 9 February and 21 February 1967, in CNA 654: 6; and Shanghai Radio, 20 February 1967, in FE 2399: B21-22.

Chapter VII Notes

1. Chang Ch'un-ch'iao, 22 October 1967, in URS 50: 18.

2. Ibid., p. 19.

3. Ibid.

4. Ibid.

5. Hunter, "The Cultural Arm," FEER 57: 22-24.

6. See Hunter, "The Cultural Arm," pp. 22-24; and WHP, 4 January 1967, in URS 46: 114-16, and SCMP(S) 162: 25-6. Power was also seized in Liberation Daily in the same fashion on January 6-- see FE 2359: B2-4.

7. See Hunter, "All-the-Way-Rebels," FEER 57: 248, where Chang is reported to have arrived on the 4th, and Esmein, p. 183, where he is reported to have flown back to Peking on the same day. Partial confirmation can be found in Chang's 22 October 1967 speech where, according to URS 50: 18, he pinpointed his date of return as April 4. We can assume that the month was incorrectly stated due to a copyist's error.

8. See WHP, 5 January 1967, in SCMP 3858: 1-4.

9. Ibid., p. 3.

10. Ibid.

11. See Hung-wei Chan-pao, 8 January 1967, in SCMP(S) 166: 1-23, for the documents generated by this rally, the official charges and penalties, and detailed accounts of what the crimes of each official

Chapter VII Notes

were reputed to be. Ch'en P'ei-hsien, kept in office here, dropped from sight after the creation of the Municipal Revolutionary Committee, to reappear only after the purge of Chang Ch'un-ch'iao a decade later--as a top Party official in Yunnan. See The Washington Post, 15 February 1977.

12. WHP, 7 January 1967, in FE 2361: B6.

13. WHP, 10 January 1967, in FE 2363: B8-10; and SCMP(S) 162: 27-28. See also WHP, 8 January 1967, in FE 2361: B6-7; and Shanghai Radio, 9 January 1967, in FE 2362: B12.

14. See, for example, Shanghai Radio, 8 January 1967, in FE 2361: B7-9; and WHP, 10 January 1967, in FE 2363: B8-10.

15. Ts'ao Ti-ch'iu, Ch'en P'ei-hsien, and Yang Hsi-kuang would thus perform the same role at the local level that Lowell Dittmer has argued Liu Shao-ch'i performed at the national level--that of a symbol towards which criticism and factional energies were to be directed. See his Liu Shao-ch'i and the Chinese Cultural Revolution.

16. See CCP Documents, p. 170.

17. See "Message of Greetings," 11 January 1967, in CB 852: 38.

18. Hunter, Shanghai Journal, p. 209.

19. Hunter, "The Cultural Arm," FEER 57: 24; Hunter, Shanghai Journal, p. 221; Chang Ch'un-ch'iao in URS 50: 19.

20. See WHP, CFJP, and Shanghai Radio, 9 January 1967, in FE 2364: B1-5. See also CB 818: 5-9, SCMP 3861: 1-4; and JPRS 40,041, pp. 14-16.

21. See NCNA, 8 January 1967, in FE 2390: B18-20; NCNA, 10 February 1967, in SCMP 3880: 25; and WHP, 10 February 1967, in FE 2392: B18-19.

22. See China News Summary (CNS) 161: 2, and White, "Shanghai's Polity," pp. 330-32.

130

23. See Hunter, Shanghai Journal, p. 239; CCP Documents, pp. 172, 175-77, 200-01, and 208.

24. See Hung-se Tsao-fan Pao, 30 January 1967, in JPRS 41,446, pp. 67-69; Shanghai Radio, 13 January 1967, in FE 2367: B6; and Peking Radio, 16 January 1967, in FE 2368: B19.

25. See Shanghai Radio, 15 January 1967, in FE 2369: B22, and Peking Radio, 16 January 1967, in FE 2368: B19. See also Mao's reference to this event in his February talks with Chang and Yao in Schram, Chairman Mao, p. 279.

26. See Chieh-fang-chün Wen-i (Liberation Army Literature), Peking, No. 2, pp. 29-30, in JPRS 42,129, pp. 26-29, and Shanghai Radio, 21 February 1967, in FE 2400: B1.

27. For the account at the docks, see Hunter, "Port in a Storm," p. 664; Shanghai Radio, 10 January 1967, in FE 2364: B11-12, and Shanghai Radio, 14 January 1967, in FE 2374: B7. For the account at the railroad terminals, see Shanghai Radio, 13 January 1967, in FE 2364: B14; NCNA, 9 February 1967, in SCMP 3880: 22-24; and Chang Ch'un-ch'iao (speech of 22 October 1967) in URS 50: 19. A Workers' Headquarters Notice was issued on 18 January 1967, nullifying raises and bonuses and ordering workers to return back pay; see CB 818: 24-26.

28. See Hung-ch'i No. 11, 1967, and JMJP, 10 July 1967, in CNA 674: 3, and Shanghai Radio, 10 January 1967, in FE 2364: B9-10.

29. See Hung-wei Chan-pao, 15 January 1967, in JPRS 40,396, pp. 16-19; Shanghai Radio, 10, 11, 12 January 1967, in FE 2363: B6; FE 2364: B12-13, B26; and FE 2365: B5-6, B13.

30. See, for example, NCNA, 16 January 1967, in FE 2370: B14-17; Shanghai Radio, 23 January 1967, in FE 2374: B6-7, and WHP, 13 February 1967, in SCMP 3889: 16-17. The gradually returning workers were often wryly referred to as "comrades who were unable to work earlier due to illness."

31. See Ezra Vogel, "Introduction," The Cultural Revolution in the Provinces, p. 6.

Chapter VII Notes

32. See Chang's talk on 22 October 1967, in URS 50: 20-21, and
    Nuova Unita in JPRS 42, 525, p. 11.

33. See Kung-jen Tsao-fan Pao, 13 March 1967, in Hunter, Shanghai
    Journal, p. 236.

34. See Ke-ming Lou, 10 March 1967, in SCMP(S) 184: 20-22, and
    Mao's mention of the opposition to the PLA at Lunghua Airfield in
    Schram, Chairman Mao, p. 278.

35. Hunter, Shanghai Journal, pp. 225-26.

36. Ibid., pp. 228-32.

37. Kung-jen Tsao-fan Pao, in Hunter, Shanghai Journal, p. 237.
    Keng's protestations about the size of Chang's support were quite
    possibly true--although quoted often in the Workers' Headquarters
    organ, statements like these were never refuted.

38. See CFJP, 3 February 1967, in FE 2394: B22-23; and Chieh-
    fang-chün Wen-i, Peking, No. 2, 1967, pp. 27-29, in JPRS
    42, 129, pp. 22-25. A directive from the Military Commission of
    the Central Committee on 28 January ordered PLA units to "more
    actively support true revolutionary leftists." See CB 852: 54-55.

39. Hunter, Shanghai Journal, p. 237, and "Yao Wen-yuan--New
    Blood in the Mao Regime," Issues and Studies 8 (March 1972):
    80-85.

40. Hunter, Shanghai Journal, p. 237.

41. See Shue, "Shanghai After the January Storm," p. 68.

42. Estimates for the Rebel numerical strength vary between six hun-
    dred thousand to one million. (See Chang Ch'un-ch'iao, in URS
    50: 18; Nuova Unita in JPRS 42,425, p. 8, and Asahi, 13 May
    1967, in DSJP, 18 May 1967, p. 15.) While these reported fig-
    ures are probably highly inflated, we can nonetheless (assuming
    that each side inflated their membership totals at roughly equal
    rates) derive an estimate of their relative strengths. If we
    assume that Scarlet strength was at eight hundred thousand, and

Chapter VII Notes

if we take one million as the correct figure for the Rebels, then the rebel faction, we assume, included approximately 56 percent of Shanghai's politically active working population. If we subtract from that one million the 520 thousand reported to have left with Keng Chin-chang and the estimated "several hundred thousand" of the Workers' Third Army (assume two hundred thousand), the Workers' Headquarters is left with less than three hundred thousand, which bears out Hunter's observation that the organization was, by late January, a mere "shell" of its former self. Even if we assume that the Workers' Headquarters' membership was swelled by the disbanding Scarlet Guards, it is difficult to imagine that the Workers' Headquarters could have comprised more than one-fourth of the city's organized workers--regardless of the actual magnitude of their numbers.

43. Shanghai Radio, 5 February 1967, in FE 2387: B12.

44. Ibid., B10-11.

45. WHP, 5 February 1967, in SCMP(S) 169: 14-19.

46. WHP, 8 February 1967, in FE 2389: B28-29.

47. Shanghai Radio, 9 February 1967, in FE 2391: B30.

48. See Chang Ch'un-ch'iao, talk on 22 October 1967, in URS 50: 21-23.

49. Kung-jen Tsao-fan Pao, 13 March 1967, in Hunter, Shanghai Journal, pp. 251-52.

50. Hunter, Shanghai Journal, pp. 254-55.

51. Mao, "Talks at Three Meetings with Comrades Chang Ch'un-ch'iao and Yao Wen-yuan," in Chairman Mao, ed. Schram, p. 277.

52. Ibid., p. 278.

53. Ibid.

54. Ibid., p. 277-78.

Chapter VII Notes

55. Ibid., p. 278. It is not clear what, if any, concrete organizational changes this name change entailed. The main pillars of Chang's power during the tenuous nineteen-day reign of the Shanghai Commune were the Military Control Commission, the Public Security Bureau, and the Workers' Headquarters--the same organizational supports Chang enjoyed before the Commune and the same institutions that remained most important on the Revolutionary Committee.

56. Shanghai Radio, 18 February 1967, in FE 2397: B14-16.

57. WHP, 19 February 1967, in SCMP(S) 168: 28-31.

58. WHP, 19 February 1967, in SCMP(S) 168: 28-29, and WHP, 22 February 1967, in SCMP(S) 169: 4-5, and in FE 2399: B22-24.

59. See Shanghai Radio, 24 February 1967, in FE 2403: B2-3; Shanghai Radio, 28 February 1967, in FE 2408: B2-3, and WHP, 27 February 1967, in FE 2403: B1-2.

60. Shanghai Radio, 24 February 1967, in FE 2401: B1.

61. See Shanghai Radio, 23 February 1967, in FE 2401: B2, and Hunter, Shanghai Journal, pp. 260-62.

62. Hunter, Shanghai Journal, pp. 260-62.

63. Alexandra Close, "Mao Plays His Last Trump," FEER, 16 March 1967, in CNI 162, and Hunter, Shanghai Journal, pp. 260-62.

64. Close, "Mao Plays His Last Trump," and Hunter, Shanghai Journal, pp. 260-62.

Chapter VIII Notes

1. Ke-ming Lou, 10 March 1967, in SCMP(S) 184: 23, and Kung-jen Tsao-fan Pao, 13 March 1967, in Hunter, Shanghai Journal, pp. 274-76.

2. See WHP, CFJP, 25 February 1967, in FE 2404: B28-31; WHP, 10 March 1967, in SCMP(S) 172: 4-6, and Hunter, Shanghai Journal, p. 263.

Chapter VIII Notes

3. WHP, 15 April 1967, in FE 2442: B15-16.

4. See CFJP, 1 May 1967, in FE 2456: B9, and also WHP, 29 April 1967, in FE 2453: B8.

5. See Shanghai Radio, 15 April 1967, in FE 2466: B22.

6. See Shanghai Radio, 8 May 1967, in FE 2463: B17; Mainichi, 10 May 1967, in DSJP, 11 May 1967, p. 19; Shanghai Radio, 13 May 1967, in FE 2467: B19-20; and Shanghai Radio, 27 May 1967, in FE 2479: B4-5.

7. See WHP, 2 April 1967, in FE 2431: B1-4, and FE 2433: B1-2; CFJP, 2 April 1967, in SCMP 3916: 23-25; CFJP, 3 April 1967, in FE 2434: B15-17; WHP, 9 April 1967, in SCMM(S) 28: 7-15; WHP, 10 April 1967, in FE 2437: B14-15; Shanghai Radio, 17 April 1967, in FE 2444: B16; Shanghai Radio, 18 April 1967, in FE 2445: B8-11; and Yomiuri, 4 April 1967, in DSJP, 4 April 1967, pp. 37-38.

8. One of the main targets of this campaign was a "reactionary" violin concerto. See WHP, 1 May 1967, in FE 2456: B11, and Shanghai Radio, 5 May 1967, in FE 2461: B6-7. See also WHP, 26 March 1967, in FE 2427: B16-19; WHP, 1 April 1967, in FE 2431: B4-6; Shanghai Radio, 12 April 1967, in FE 2443: B15; Shanghai Radio, 8 June 1967, in FE 2489: B11-12, and Chang Ch'un-ch'iao, in SCMM 651: 16.

9. See CCP Documents, pp. 497-98.

10. See WHP, 11 March 1967, in SCMP 3902: 19-20, and CFJP, 11 March 1967, in SCMP 3904: 14-16.

11. See WHP, 6 March 1967, in SCMP 3897: 3-5, and in JPRS 41,450, pp. 124-25; WHP, 7 March 1967, in FE 2412: B24-26; Shanghai Radio, 8 March 1967, in FE 2414: B4-5; and CFJP, 15 March 1967, in SCMP 3904: 14. See the relevant Central directives in CCP Documents, p. 570, and SCMM(S) 17: 67.

12. See WHP, 6 January 1967, in FE 2361: B4-5.

Chapter VIII Notes

13. See Nuova Unita in JPRS 42,525, p. 15; Hung-se Tsao-fan Pao, 30 January 1967, in JPRS 41,446, pp. 65-69; and Hunter, Shanghai Journal, pp. 207, 223.

14. CNS 154: A8-9.

15. See WHP, 17 February 1967, in SCMP(S) 170: 11-13.

16. See WHP, 19 February 1967, in URS 47: 138-143; WHP, 4 February 1967, in FE 2388: B2-3, and SCMP(S) 170: 9-10; WHP, 21 February 1967, in SCMP(S) 167: 36-39; and WHP, 6 March 1967, in URS 47, pp. 144-47.

17. See NCNA, 24 March 1967 (from Shanghai Physical Culture Fighting Bulletin), in FE 2428: B21-23.

18. CFJP, 19 February 1967, in FE 2402: B6-7, and WHP, 24 February 1967, in FE 2403: B10-12.

19. WHP, 12 February 1967, in FE 2395: B39-41. Apparently the identical charge made earlier against the leadership of the old MPC was excluded from this reformulation.

20. WHP, 18 February 1967, in SCMP 3892: 6-8, and WHP, 13 February 1967, in SCMP 3888: 23-26.

21. WHP, 21 February 1967, in SCMP(S) 170: 14-15; CFJP, 16 March 1967, in FE 2430: B6-7; and Hunter, "Three Cadres of Shanghai," FEER 56: 491-95.

22. See WHP, 7 March and 10 March 1967, in FE 2414: B1-2; WHP, CFJP, 3 April 1967, in FE 2436: B17-18; and WHP, 7 April 1967, in FE 2436: B9-11.

23. See WHP, 12 April 1967, in SCMP 3925: 32-34, and WHP, CFJP, 29 April 1967, in FE 2456: B10-11.

24. WHP, 15 January 1967, in Esmcin, The Chinese Cultural Revolution, p. 131.

25. WHP, 18 February 1967, in URS 47: 39-40.

136

Chapter VIII Notes

26. WHP, 13 February 1967, in URS 47: 160-62, and WHP, 27 February 1967, in FE 2407: B36.

27. See WHP, 15 February 1967, in FE 2393: B8-9; WHP, 16 February 1967, in URS 47: 154-57; and WHP, 18 February 1967, in URS 47: 157-58.

28. "Comrade Chang Ch'un-ch'iao's Speech at Chiao-t'ung University of Shanghai," Tzu-liao chuan-chi (Special Collection of Information Material) Canton, 10 February 1968, in SCMP 4146: 3.

29. WHP, 17 February 1967, in URS 47: 31-34, and SCMP(S) 170: 16-22.

30. WHP, 17 February 1967, in URS 47: 34-38.

31. WHP, 3 March 1967, in SCMP(S) 171: 14-15.

32. See WHP, 8 February 1967, in FE 2391: B30-31; WHP, 12 February 1967, in FE 2392: B16-17, and CFJP, 28 February 1967, in SCMP(S) 178: 17-20.

33. Shanghai Radio, 15 February 1967, in FE 2395: B31-33.

34. CCP Documents, pp. 301-02.

35. See WHP, 16 February 1967, in URS 47: 180-81, and in SCMP(S) 168: 27. See also CNA 654: 4.

36. See WHP, 12 February 1967, in URS 47: 168-70, 176-78, and CFJP, 16 February 1967, in SCMP(S) 176: 12-16.

37. See WHP, 25 January 1967, in URS 47: 174-76. See also WHP, 20 January 1967, in URS 47: 178-80; WHP, 25 January 1967, in Current Scene, 15 March 1968, p. 19, and WHP, 25 February 1968, in SCMP 4146: 15-16.

38. Shanghai Radio, 27 February 1967, in FE 2404: B35.

39. FE 2359: B3.

Chapter VIII Notes

40. Canton Physical Culture Fighting Front, in SCMP 3913, and Current Scene, 15 March 1968, p. 27.

41. WHP, 30 January 1967, in SCMP(S) 168: 13-14.

42. CCP Documents, pp. 305-06.

43. Shanghai Radio, 27 February 1967, in FE 2404: B35, and WHP, 28 February 1967, in SCMP(S) 174: 6-7, 12.

44. Shanghai Radio, 1 March 1967, in FE 2408: B1.

45. WHP, 18 January 1967, in FE 2372: B21.

46. See Shanghai Radio, 28 January 1967, in FE 2380: B28-30; NCNA, 30 January 1967, in CB 818: 21-23; WHP, 12 February 1967, in SCMP(S) 167: 32-33; and WHP, 19 February 1967, in SCMP(S) 167: 34-35. See also CCP Documents, pp. 313-14.

47. WHP, 9 February 1967, in FE 2390: B15-16.

48. See WHP, 11 February 1967, in SCMP(S) 168: 24, and WHP, 12 February 1967, in CNA 654: 2.

49. See Shanghai Radio, 9 February 1967, in FE 2392: B21.

50. Shanghai Radio, 28 February 1967, in FE 2405: B28-30, and WHP, 1 March 1967, in SCMP(S) 171: 25-26.

51. WHP, 1 March 1967, in SCMP(S) 171: 21-24.

52. Ke-ming Lou, 10 March 1967, in SCMP(S) 184: 18-19.

53. See WHP, 5 February 1967, in FE 2389: B37-38; WHP, 9 February 1967, in FE 2390: B15-16; and Shanghai Radio, 9 February 1967, in FE 2392: B21. See also SCMP(S) 167: 18-24.

54. WHP, 5 February 1967, in FE 2389: B37-38.

55. See Hunter, "The Cultural Arm," FEER 57: 24, and WHP, 1 March 1967, in SCMP(S) 171: 21-24.

138

Chapter VIII Notes

56. See CNA 654: 2, and Hunter, Shanghai Journal, pp. 248-49.

57. See Ke-ming Lou, 10 March 1967, in SCMP(S) 184: 18-19; Shanghai Radio, 28 February 1967, in FE 2405: B28-30; and WHP, 1 March 1967, in SCMP(S) 171: 20-21, 25-26.

58. See WHP, 11 February 1967, in CNA 654: 2; Shanghai Radio, 11 February 1967, in FE 2393: B10-13; and WHP, 1 March 1967, in SCMP(S) 171: 21-24.

59. See Shanghai Radio, 21 February 1967, in FE 2400: B1-2, and Shanghai Radio, 24 February 1967, in FE 2402: B3-4.

60. Shanghai Radio, 29 March 1967, in FE 2430: B8-9.

61. See Thomas W. Robinson, "The Wuhan Incident: Local Strife and Provincial Rebellion During the Cultural Revolution," CQ 47 (July-September 1971): 413-38.

62. See Robinson, "The Wuhan Incident," p. 422.

63. See Barry Burton, "The Cultural Revolution's Ultraleft Conspiracy: The 'May 16 Group'," Asian Survey (AS) 11 (November 1971): 1029-53; and Harvey Nelsen, "Military Forces in the Cultural Revolution," CQ 51 (July-September 1972): 444-74, 460-62.

64. See, for example, Victor C. Falkenheim, "The Cultural Revolution in Kwangsi, Yunnan, and Fukien," AS 9 (August 1969): 580-97; Deborah S. Davis, "The Cultural Revolution in Wuhan," in The Cultural Revolution in the Provinces, pp. 147-70; Thomas J. Mathews, "The Cultural Revolution in Szechwan," in The Cultural Revolution in the Provinces, pp. 94-142; and Jürgen Domes, "Generals and Red Guards--the Role of Huang Yung-sheng and the Canton Military Command in the Kwangtung Cultural Revolution," Asia Quarterly 1-2 (1971): 3-31, 123-59.

65. See Robinson, "The Wuhan Incident," pp. 436-37, Nelsen, "Military Forces," pp. 460-62, Burton, "The 'May 16 Group'," p. 1043, and Jürgen Domes, "The Cultural Revolution and the Army," AS 8 (May 1968): 349-63, 358-59.

Chapter VIII Notes

66. See Issues and Studies (Supplement) 1 (7 February 1968): 24.
Liao thus ranked alongside Yao Wen-yuan and Wang Shao-yung.

67. See "Chang Ch'un-ch'iao's Rise to Power During the Cultural
Revolution," Issues and Studies (Supplement) 2 (5 March 1969):
15-18, 15.

68. Nelsen, "Military Forces," pp. 460-61.

69. See Shanghai Radio, 22 July 1967, in FE 2525: B22.

70. See the two editorial broadcasts over Shanghai Radio, 20 July
1967, in FE 2526: B22-25.

71. See Shanghai Radio, 28 July 1967, in FE 2535: B2.

72. See the editorial entitled "Remain at Ease while Clouds of Chaos
Pass By," Shanghai Radio, 30 July 1967, in FE 2533: B11-12.

73. See Shanghai Radio, 1 August 1967, in FE 2535: B3-4.

74. Ibid., B4-5.

75. Ibid., B4.

76. Ibid., B5.

77. See the sensationalized description broadcast over Shanghai Radio
on 4 August 1967, in FE 2536: B3-5.

78. See FE 2536: B5-10.

79. CFJP, 4 August 1967, in FE 2536: B10.

80. See CFJP, 5 August 1967, in FE 2357: B17-19; Shanghai Radio,
6 August 1967, in FE 2537: B21-24. The resolution of the Municipal Revolutionary Committee, broadcast over Shanghai Radio on
6 August 1967, is in FE 2538: B15-19.

81. Shanghai Radio, 13 August 1967, in FE 2546: B20-24.

140

82. See the following Shanghai Radio reports: 7 August 1967, in FE
    2540: B6-8; 8 August, in FE 2540: B20-24; 9 August, in FE 2544:
    B34-38; and 13 August, in FE 2546: B20-24.

83. See Yao Wen-yuan, "Comment on T'ao Chu's Two Books," Hung-
    Ch'i, 17 September 1967, and Burton, "The 'May 16 Group'."
    pp. 1043-44, 1046-47.

Chapter IX Notes

1. In addition to the various interpretations of the Cultural Revolution in Shanghai cited in Chapter I above, general accounts for
   China as a whole also reflect this perspective. Parris Chang has
   forwarded a scenario of conflict between the CCRG and local leaders where the provincial officials engage in "deceptive" and "eva-
   sive" attempts to preserve their power, using, among other tactics,
   financial resources to "buy off" workers. See Parris Chang,
   "The Role of Ch'en Po-ta in the Cultural Revolution," Asia Quarterly 2 (1973): 17-58, 34-35, and "Provincial Party Leaders'
   Strategies," pp. 524-25. Ezra Vogel, in an analysis written within
   months of the events themselves, presents a parallel interpretation.
   In his "The Structure of Conflict" in The Cultural Revolution:
   1967 in Review, he argues that "anti-Maoists" in the provincial
   leadership waged a form of "guerilla war" against Cultural Revolution policies by encouraging strikes among workers, disrupting
   industrial, communication, and transport work, by inciting industrial workers to request higher wages, and by dividing the Red
   Guard movement and stirring up factionalism (p. 107). All of
   these are presented as defensive moves designed to "slow down
   and sabotage" the Cultural Revolution.
        Neale Hunter, in his own account for Shanghai, concludes that
   the MPC had manipulated conservative forces and had blackmailed
   and intimidated dissident students and workers (pp. 294-95),
   despite considerable evidence to the contrary in his own narrative--
   a discrepancy which Lynn T. White III has also noted ("Leadership in Shanghai," p. 350).

2. Thus, Parris Chang explains, the CCRG, seeing that the Cultural Revolution was making little headway, dispatched Chang
   Ch'un-ch'iao and Yao Wen-yuan to Shanghai in order to "direct

Chapter IX Notes

and coordinate the rebels' attacks on Shanghai Party authorities" ("The Role of Ch'en Po-ta," pp. 35, 38). He interprets the January Revolution in a way diametrically opposed to the interpretation forwarded here--in the face of economic breakdown, he asserts, "the Maoist leadership decided not to retreat, but to take the most extreme measures yet." ("Provincial Party Leaders' Strategies," p. 526).

3. See, for example, Parris Chang, "Ch'en Po-ta's Role," pp. 37-39.

4. See the sources cited in footnote 1 above, and in Chapter I above.

5. The work of Lynn T. White III and Michel Oksenberg is instructive here. White lays out the stratification within the working class that developed during the early 1960s, and notes that differences within plants and between shops of varying labor productivities, many of which employed a mix of permanent and nonpermanent labor, possibly set the sociological foundations of mass factionalism. Oksenberg, in his "Occupational Groups," sketches out the structure of benefits among various sections of the working population and, especially important for our analysis, reminds us that a natural harmony existed between the interests of permanent workers and lower level management, both of whose benefits were tied to continued industrial progress. Hong Yung Lee's "The Radical Students in Kwangtung during the Cultural Revolution," and his forthcoming book based on his Ph.D. dissertation, solidly document the link between class background and political orientation during the Cultural Revolution.

6. Forwarded by "romantic ideologues," Parris Chang argues, the Shanghai Commune was a reminder of "the power of ideology in Chinese politics." ("The Role of Ch'en Po-ta," pp. 37, 39.)

7. See, for example, Goldman, "China's Anti-Confucian Campaign, 1973-74," CQ 63 (September 1975): 435-62, 435-37, where she reasons that since the Anti-Confucian campaign seemed aimed at producing "unity and stability," it must have been directed by Chou En-lai and the "moderates" against the "disruptive groups that emerged from the Cultural Revolution"--"radical ideologues" like Chang Ch'un-ch'iao (p. 435).

SOURCES

Newspapers and Periodicals

American Political Science Review

Asahi, Tokyo

Asia Quarterly

Asian Survey

Chieh-fang, Shanghai

Chieh-fang Chün Wen-i, Peking

Chieh-fang Jih-pao, Shanghai

China Reconstructs, Peking

China Quarterly

Current Scene, Hong Kong

Eastern Horizon, Hong Kong

Far Eastern Economic Review, Hong Kong

Hai-kang Chan-pao, Shanghai (RG)*

Hsueh-hsi yü p'i-p'an, Shanghai

Hsin-min Wan-pao, Shanghai

Hsin-wen Chan-shih, Shanghai (RG)

Hung-ch'i, Peking

Hung-kung Chan-pao, Shanghai (RG)

Hung se Tsau-fan Pao, Shanghai (RG)

*(RG) indicates Red Guard Publications

Hung-wei Chan-pao, Shanghai (RG)

Issues and Studies, Taipei

Issues and Studies (Supplement), Taipei

Jen-min Jih-pao, Peking

Journal of Asian Studies

Ke-ming Lou, Shanghai (RG)

Ke-ming Tsao-fan Pao, Shanghai (RG)

Kuai Pao, Hong Kong

Kuang-ming Jih-pao, Peking

Kung-jen Jih-pao, Peking

Kung-jen Tsao-fan Pao, Shanghai (RG)

Mainichi, Tokyo

Nihon Kezai, Tokyo

Nuova Unita, Rome

Pei-ching Jih-pao, Peking

Peking Review

Sankei, Tokyo

Shang-hai Kung-shang, Shanghai

Shang-hai Wen-hsueh, Shanghai

Sing Tao Daily, Hong Kong

South China Morning Post, Hong Kong

Ta Kung Pao, Peking

Ta-p'i-p'an T'ung-hsun, Canton (RG)

Tokyo Shimbun, Tokyo

Tzu-liao chuan-chi, Canton (RG)

Washington Post

Wen-hui Pao, Shanghai

Yomiuri, Tokyo

Translation and Broadcast Monitoring Services

British Broadcasting Corporation, Summary of World Broadcasts (Far East)

China News Analysis

China News Items from the Press

China News Summary

Current Background

Czechoslovak Press Service

Daily Summary of the Japanese Press

Foreign Broadcast Information Service, Daily Report (Far East)

Joint Publications Research Service

Selections from China Mainland Magazines

Selections from China Mainland Magazines (Supplement)

Selections from People's Republic of China Magazines

Survey of the China Mainland Press

Survey of the China Mainland Press (Supplement)

Union Research Service

Union Research Service Biographical Service

Articles

Anderson, Evelyn. "Shanghai: The Masses Unleashed." Problems of Communism 47 (January–February 1968): 12–28.

Burton, Barry. "The Cultural Revolution's Ultraleft Conspiracy: The 'May 16 Group.'" Asian Survey 11 (November 1971): 1029–53.

Chang, Parris H. "The Role of Ch'en Po-ta in the Cultural Revolution." Asia Quarterly 1 (1973): 17–58.

_____. "Provincial Party Leaders' Strategies for Survival during the Cultural Revolution." In Elites in the People's Republic of China, edited by R. Scalapino, pp. 501–39. Seattle: University of Washington Press, 1972.

146

Davis, Deborah S. "The Cultural Revolution in Wuhan." In The Cultural Revolution in the Provinces, pp. 147-70, Harvard East Asian Monographs. Cambridge: Harvard East Asian Research Center, 1971.

Dirlik, Arif. "National Development and Social Revolution in Early Chinese Marxist Thought." China Quarterly 57 (April-May 1974): 286-309.

Dittmer, Lowell. "Thought Reform and Cultural Revolution: An Analysis of the Symbolism of Chinese Polemics." American Political Science Review 71 (March 1977): 67-85.

Domes, Jürgen. "Generals and Red Guards--The Role of Huang Yung-sheng and the Canton Military Area Command in the Kwangtung Cultural Revolution." Asia Quarterly 1 (1971): 3-31; 2 (1971): 123-59.

_____. "The Cultural Revolution and the Army." Asian Survey 8 (May 1968): 349-63.

Falkenheim, Victor C. "The Cultural Revolution in Kwangsi, Yunnan and Fukien." Asian Survey 9 (August 1969): 580-97.

Goldman, Merle. "China's Anti-Confucian Campaign, 1973-74." China Quarterly 63 (September 1975): 435-62.

_____. "The Chinese Communist Party's 'Cultural Revolution' of 1962-64." In Ideology and Politics in Contemporary China, edited by Chalmers Johnson, pp. 219-54. Seattle: University of Washington Press, 1973.

_____. "Party Policies Towards the Intellectuals: The Unique Blooming and Contending of 1961-62." In Party Leadership and Revolutionary Power in China, edited by John W. Lewis, pp. 268-303. London: Cambridge University Press, 1970.

Lee, Hong Yung. "The Radical Students in Kwangtung During the Cultural Revolution." China Quarterly 64 (December 1975): 645-83.

Mathews, Thomas J. "The Cultural Revolution in Szechwan." In The Cultural Revolution in the Provinces, pp. 94-142, Harvard East Asian Monographs. Cambridge: Harvard East Asian Research Center, 1971.

Munro, Donald. "The Yang Hsien-chen Affair." China Quarterly 22
(April-June 1965): 75-82.

Nee, Victor. "Revolution and Bureaucracy: Shanghai in the Cultural
Revolution." In China's Uninterrupted Revolution, edited by
Victor Nee and James Peck, pp. 322-414. New York: Pantheon,
1975.

Nelsen, Harvey. "Military Forces in the Cultural Revolution." China
Quarterly 51 (July-September 1972): 444-74.

Oksenberg, Michel. "Getting Ahead and Along in Communist China:
The Ladder of Success on the Eve of the Cultural Revolution." In
Party Leadership and Revolutionary Power in China, edited by
John W. Lewis, pp. 304-50. London: Cambridge University
Press, 1970.

_____. "Occupational Groups in Chinese Society and the
Cultural Revolution." In The Cultural Revolution: 1967 in Review,
pp. 1-44, Michigan Papers in Chinese Studies, vol. 2. Ann Arbor:
University of Michigan Center for Chinese Studies, 1968.

Robinson, Thomas W. "The Wuhan Incident: Local Strife and Provincial Rebellion During the Cultural Revolution." China Quarterly
47 (July-September 1971): 413-38.

Shue, Vivienne B. "Shanghai After the January Storm." In The Cultural
Revolution in the Provinces, pp. 66-93, Harvard East Asian
Monographs. Cambridge: Harvard East Asian Research Center,
1971.

Tang Tsou. "The Cultural Revolution and the Chinese Political System."
China Quarterly 38 (April-June 1969): 63-91.

Tannenbaum, Gerald. "The 1967 Shanghai January Revolution Recounted." Eastern Horizon 7 (May-June 1968): 7-25.

Vogel, Ezra F. "The Structure of Conflict: China in 1967." In The
Cultural Revolution: 1967 in Review, pp. 97-125, Michigan Papers
in Chinese Studies, vol. 2. Ann Arbor: University of Michigan
Center for Chinese Studies, 1968.

White, Lynn T., III. "Workers Politics in Shanghai." Journal of Asian
Studies 36 (November 1976): 99-116.

White, Lynn T., III. "Local Autonomy in China During the Cultural Revolution." American Political Science Review 70 (June 1976): 479-91.

_____. "Leadership in Shanghai, 1955-69." In Elites in the People's Republic of China, edited by Robert A. Scalapino, pp. 302-77. Seattle: University of Washington Press, 1972.

_____. "Practice and Theory: The Contract Proletariat." Mimeographed. Hong Kong: The University of Hong Kong Centre of Asian Studies, 1972.

_____. "Shanghai's Polity in Cultural Revolution." In The City in Communist China, edited by John W. Lewis, pp. 325-70. Stanford: Stanford University Press, 1971.

Books

Ansley, Clive. The Heresy of Wu Han. Toronto: University of Toronto Press, 1971.

Bennett, Gordon A. and Ronald N. Montaperto. Red Guard: The Political Biography of Dai Hsiao-ai. Garden City, N.Y.: Anchor, 1972.

Boorman, Howard L., ed. Biographical Dictionary of Republican China. 4 vols. New York: Columbia University Press, 1967.

CCP Documents of the Great Proletarian Cultural Revolution. Hong Kong: Union Research Institute, 1968.

Chang, Parris. Radicals and Radical Ideology in the Cultural Revolution. New York: Research Institute on Communist Affairs, Columbia University, 1972.

Chen, Jack. Inside the Cultural Revolution. New York: Macmillan, 1975.

Chen, Theodore H. E. Thought Reform of the Chinese Intellectuals. Hong Kong: Hong Kong University Press, 1960.

The Cultural Revolution: 1967 in Review. Michigan Papers in Chinese Studies, vol. 2. Ann Arbor: University of Michigan Center for Chinese Studies, 1968.

The Cultural Revolution in the Provinces. Harvard East Asian Mono-
    graphs. Cambridge: Harvard East Asian Research Center, 1971.

Daubier, Jean. A History of the Chinese Cultural Revolution. New
    York: Vintage, 1974.

Dittmer, Lowell. Liu Shao-ch'i and the Chinese Cultural Revolution:
    The Politics of Mass Criticism. Berkeley: University of Cali-
    fornia Press, 1974.

Esmein, Jean. The Chinese Cultural Revolution. Garden City, N.Y.:
    Anchor, 1973.

Feuerwerker, Albert and S. Cheng. Chinese Communist Studies of
    Modern Chinese History. Harvard East Asian Monographs.
    Cambridge: Harvard East Asian Research Center, 1961.

Feuerwerker, Albert, ed. History in Communist China. Cambridge:
    Harvard University Press, 1968.

Fokkema, D. W. Literary Doctrine in China and Soviet Influence, 1956-
    1960. The Hague: Mouton, 1965.

Goldman, Merle. Literary Dissent in Communist China. New York:
    Atheneum, 1971.

The Great Cultural Revolution in China. Hong Kong: Asia Research
    Centre, 1967.

Hunter, Neale. Shanghai Journal: An Eyewitness Account of the Cul-
    tural Revolution. Boston: Beacon, 1969.

Johnson, Chalmers, ed. Ideology and Politics in Contemporary China.
    Seattle: University of Washington Press, 1973.

Karol, K. S. The Second Chinese Revolution. New York: Hill and
    Wang, 1974.

Klein, Donald W. and Anne B. Clark. Biographic Dictionary of Chinese
    Communism, 1921-1965. 2 vols. Cambridge: Harvard University
    Press, 1971.

Knight, Sophia. Window on Shanghai: Letters from China, 1965-67.
    London: Andre Deutsch, 1967.

Lang, Olga. Pa Chin and his Writings. Cambridge: Harvard University Press, 1972.

Lee, Hong Yung. "The Political Mobilization of the Red Guards and Revolutionary Rebels in the Cultural Revolution." Ph.D. dissertation, University of Chicago, 1975.

Lewis, John W., ed. The City in Communist China. Stanford: Stanford University Press, 1971.

_____, ed. Party Leadership and Revolutionary Power in China. London: Cambridge University Press, 1970.

Lieberthal, Kenneth. A Research Guide to Central Party and Government Meetings in China, 1949-1975. White Plains, N.Y.: International Arts and Sciences Press, 1976.

MacFarquhar, Roderick. The Origins of the Cultural Revolution, Volume 1: Contradictions among the People, 1956-1957. New York: Columbia University Press, 1974.

_____. The Hundred Flowers Campaign and the Chinese Intellectuals. New York: Praeger, 1960.

Nee, Victor and James Peck, eds. China's Uninterrupted Revolution: From 1840 to the Present. New York: Pantheon, 1975.

Pusey, James. The Wu Han Campaign. Harvard East Asian Monographs. Cambridge: Harvard East Asian Research Center, 1969.

Scalapino, Robert, ed. Elites in the People's Republic of China. Seattle: University of Washington Press, 1972.

Schram, Stuart R. Chairman Mao Talks to the People: Talks and Letters, 1956-1971. New York: Pantheon, 1974.

Singer, Martin. Educated Youth and the Cultural Revolution in China. Michigan Papers in Chinese Studies, vol. 10. Ann Arbor: University of Michigan Center for Chinese Studies, 1971.

Solomon, Richard H. Mao's Revolution and the Chinese Political Culture. Berkeley: University of California Press, 1971.

Who's Who in Communist China. 2 vols. Hong Kong: Union Research Institute, 1969.

MICHIGAN PAPERS IN CHINESE STUDIES

No. 2. The Cultural Revolution: 1967 in Review, four essays by Michel Oksenberg, Carl Riskin, Robert Scalapino, and Ezra Vogel.

No. 3. Two Studies in Chinese Literature, by Li Chi and Dale Johnson.

No. 4. Early Communist China: Two Studies, by Ronald Suleski and Daniel Bays.

No. 5. The Chinese Economy, ca. 1870-1911, by Albert Feuerwerker.

No. 6. Chinese Paintings in Chinese Publications, 1956-1968: An Annotated Bibliography and an Index to the Paintings, by E. J. Laing.

No. 7. The Treaty Ports and China's Modernization: What Went Wrong? by Rhoads Murphey.

No. 8. Two Twelfth Century Texts on Chinese Painting, by Robert J. Maeda.

No. 9. The Economy of Communist China, 1949-1969, by Chu-yuan Cheng.

No. 10. Educated Youth and the Cultural Revolution in China, by Martin Singer.

No. 11. Premodern China: A Bibliographical Introduction, by Chun-shu Chang.

No. 12. Two Studies on Ming History, by Charles O. Hucker.

No. 13. Nineteenth Century China: Five Imperialist Perspectives, selected by Dilip Basu, edited by Rhoads Murphey.

No. 14. Modern China, 1840-1972: An Introduction to Sources and Research Aids, by Andrew J. Nathan.

No. 15. Women in China: Studies in Social Change and Feminism, edited by Marilyn B. Young.

No. 16. An Annotated Bibliography of Chinese Painting Catalogues and Related Texts, by Hin-cheung Lovell.

No. 17. China's Allocation of Fixed Capital Investment, 1952-1957, by Chu-yuan Cheng.

No. 18. Health, Conflict, and the Chinese Political System, by David M. Lampton.

No. 19. Chinese and Japanese Music-Dramas, edited by J. I. Crump and William P. Malm.

MICHIGAN ABSTRACTS OF CHINESE AND
JAPANESE WORKS ON CHINESE HISTORY

NONSERIES PUBLICATION

Index to the "Chan-kuo Ts'e," by Sharon Fidler and J. I. Crump. A
companion volume to the Chan-kuo Ts'e, translated by J. I. Crump
(Oxford: Clarendon Press, 1970).

Michigan Papers and Abstracts available from:

Center for Chinese Studies
The University of Michigan
Lane Hall (Publications)
Ann Arbor, MI 48109 USA

Prepaid Orders Only
write for complete price listing

Printed and bound by CPI Group (UK) Ltd, Croydon, CR0 4YY

13/04/2025

14656508-0005